First World War
and Army of Occupation
War Diary
France, Belgium and Germany

59 DIVISION
178 Infantry Brigade
Northumberland Fusiliers
36th Battalion (Territorial)
18 April 1918 - 31 May 1919

WO95/3025/11

The Naval & Military Press Ltd
www.nmarchive.com
Published in association with The National Archives

Published by

The Naval & Military Press Ltd

Unit 10 Ridgewood Industrial Park,

Uckfield, East Sussex,

TN22 5QE England

Tel: +44 (0) 1825 749494

www.naval-military-press.com

www.nmarchive.com

This diary has been reprinted in facsimile from the original. Any imperfections are inevitably reproduced and the quality may fall short of modern type and cartographic standards.

© Crown Copyright
Images reproduced by permission of The National Archives, London, England, 2015.

Contents

Document type	Place/Title	Date From	Date To
Heading	WO 3025 59 Div 178 1.B 36th Bn Northumberland Fus. 1918 Apr-1919 May		
Heading	59th Division 178th Infy Bde 36th Bn Northumberland Fus. Apr 1918-May 1919.		
War Diary	Margate.	18/04/1918	06/05/1918
War Diary	Calais.	07/05/1918	09/05/1918
War Diary	Bailleul-Lez-Pernes Sheet 36 B. A 21d 3.2.	10/05/1918	11/05/1918
War Diary	St Leonard. I 6 A Central	12/05/1918	21/05/1918
War Diary	Bois Des Rietz I 12d 4.1.	22/05/1918	31/05/1918
Heading	War Diary Of 36 Gn. Bn Northumberland Fusiliers For June 1918		
Miscellaneous	178th Infantry Bgde	30/06/1918	30/06/1918
War Diary	Bois De Rietz I 12b 4.1 Sheet 44 B	01/06/1918	15/06/1918
War Diary	W 23 C 6.6. Sheet 44 B.	16/06/1918	16/06/1918
War Diary	Predefin 6 D11 Hazebranch Sheet 5a	17/06/1918	30/06/1918
Heading	War Diary 36th Bn North'd Fusiliers. July 1918 Vol 4		
War Diary	Predefin Sheet 44 C F22d 5.1.	01/07/1918	22/07/1918
War Diary	Sheet 51c.p.18.d.Gouy En Artois	23/07/1918	31/07/1918
Heading	War Diary 36th Northumberland Fus. For August 1918. Vol 5		
War Diary	Gouy-En-Artois P.18.C.Sheet 51C	01/08/1918	02/08/1918
War Diary	Mercatel Switch Support. M.4.a.2.4 Sheet 5lb. S.W.	03/08/1918	09/08/1918
War Diary	Brickfields S.2.b.52.	10/08/1918	13/08/1918
War Diary	Bellacourt Sheet 51C SE R S1	14/08/1918	14/08/1918
War Diary	Bellacourt Sheet 51C SE R S1	15/08/1918	17/08/1918
War Diary	Barly P 15 Sheet 51cse P15c 95.75.	18/08/1918	19/08/1918
War Diary	Barly Sheet 51cse X4d 4.6	21/08/1918	22/08/1918
War Diary	Saulty. Lens II 4g Central	23/08/1918	23/08/1918
War Diary	Manqueville Sheet 36a Edition 6.U 3 B.	24/08/1918	24/08/1918
War Diary	Manqueville Sheet 36a Edition 6.U 3 B.	25/08/1918	26/08/1918
War Diary	Robecq P23d8.2 Sheet 36a Edition 6	27/08/1918	27/08/1918
War Diary	Robecq P23d8.2 Sheet 36a Edition 6	28/08/1918	28/08/1918
War Diary	Robecq	29/08/1918	29/08/1918
War Diary	Robecq Sheet 36a Q18,c,40.20.	30/08/1918	31/08/1918
Heading	War Diary Of 36th Bn Northumberland Fusiliers September 1918.		
Miscellaneous	178th Infantry Brigade.	30/09/1918	30/09/1918
War Diary	Sheet 36a Q18c 40.20	01/09/1918	01/09/1918
War Diary	Sheet 36a R15d 40.95.	02/09/1918	02/09/1918
War Diary	R.18c 25,20	03/09/1918	03/09/1918
War Diary	M 14.c.50.00	04/09/1918	07/09/1918
War Diary	M.11.b.95.87	08/09/1918	09/09/1918
War Diary	M.14 A.20.30	10/09/1918	21/09/1918
War Diary	M12a.50.90 Sheet 36 Sw1.	22/09/1918	28/09/1918
War Diary	Sheet 36a.S.E.2 R. 3.d.40.10.	29/09/1918	30/09/1918
Heading	War Diary 36th N F's War Diary Octr 1918 Vol 7		
Miscellaneous	178th Inf. Bde.	31/10/1918	31/10/1918
War Diary	Pontriquel R.3.d.40.10 Sheet 36a. S.E.2.	01/10/1918	02/10/1918
War Diary	E.18.a.2.1. Sheet 36 N.W. H.18.a.20.10.	03/10/1918	03/10/1918
War Diary	H.26.a.60.50.	04/10/1918	10/10/1918

Type	Description	From	To
War Diary	I.32.c.40.00 Sheet 36 N.W.	11/10/1918	14/10/1918
War Diary	H.27.d.10.85.	15/10/1918	15/10/1918
War Diary	I.33.b.50.75.	16/10/1918	16/10/1918
War Diary	I 36b.55.70.	16/10/1918	16/10/1918
War Diary	Lomme J.27.c.40.25. Sheet 36 N.E.3.	17/10/1918	17/10/1918
War Diary	Flers. Tournai Sheet 5. 5.A.5.6.	18/10/1918	18/10/1918
War Diary	Templeuve H.33a.74. Sheet 37	19/10/1918	19/10/1918
Miscellaneous	0000 Should Read		
War Diary	Templeuve, H.33a.7.4.Sheet 37.	19/10/1918	19/10/1918
War Diary	H.30.d.00.40 Sheet 37.	20/10/1918	20/10/1918
War Diary	H.30.d.00.40 Sheet 37	20/10/1918	21/10/1918
War Diary	Nechin H.14.c.70.60.	22/10/1918	24/10/1918
War Diary	Nechin H.14.c.7.6. Sheet 37.	24/10/1918	24/10/1918
War Diary	Toufflers E.22.6.4.4. Sheet 37.	25/10/1918	31/10/1918
Heading	War Diary 36th Batt. Northumberland Fuslrs. November 1918.		
War Diary	Toufflers G.22.b.4.4 Sheet 37.	02/11/1918	07/11/1918
War Diary	Hulans H.20.d.50.80.	08/11/1918	08/11/1918
War Diary	Burgogne J.15.d.70.60.	09/11/1918	09/11/1918
War Diary	Anuaing L.i.c.10.40.	10/11/1918	11/11/1918
War Diary	Leuze.	12/11/1918	18/11/1918
War Diary	Kain	18/11/1918	19/11/1918
War Diary	Templeuve	19/11/1918	19/11/1918
War Diary	Petit Ronchin	20/11/1918	30/11/1918
Miscellaneous	The Gap Between November 1918 And May 1919 Has Been Noted		
Heading	War Diary May 1919 36th Battalion Northumberland Fusiliers		
War Diary	Dunkerque	01/05/1919	31/05/1919

WO 3025
50 Div 178 I.B.
36th Bn Northumberland Fus.
1918 Apr - 19th May

59TH DIVISION
178TH INFY BDE

36TH BN NOTHUMBERLAND FUS.
APR 1918-MAY 1919

From UR

WAR DIARY
INTELLIGENCE SUMMARY

Army Form C. 2118.

Place	Date	Hour	Summary of Events and Information	Remarks and references to Appendices
MARGATE.	18/4/18 April 18		War Office telegram states that 36th Bn N.F. will be mobilized forthwith at MARGATE as a Garrison Battn for service in France at War establishment Part VII A Table S.D. 2 Feb 27: 1918.	
"	22/4/18		Following drafts reported from 3rd Line:– 5 Sergeants, 3 C/Cospls, + 12 men. Total 20. From 3rd Battn NF 14 Scpls, 4 L/Cpls, 11 Cpls. 16 C/Cpls, + 130 men. Total 195	9am.
"	23/4/18		The following drafts reported:–	8am.

	Sergts	Cspls	L/Cpls	Pts	Total
3rd N.F.	2	–	3	18	23
4th N.F.	1	–	–	17	18
51st N.F.	1	–	–	18	18 ?
4th Lincs	1	1	–	3	5
3rd Leicesters	1	–	–	8	8
51st Leicesters.	1	–	1	4	4
52nd Leicesters	1	–	–	7	7
3rd S. Staffs.	1	–	–	12	13
3rd Notts & Derby.	1	2	4	7	14
4th Notts & Derby.	2	1	1	8	11
5 2nd N/th &Derby.				1	1
					122

| " | 24/4/18 | | The following drafts reported:– | 8am. |

	Sergts	Cspls	L/Cpls	Pts	Total
3rd Leicesters	2	–	–	13	15
5th S. Staffs.	1	–	–	8	8
5th Notts & Derbys.	1	–	2	9	12
5th Royal Fusiliers.	5	7	5	58	75
					110

Army Form C. 2118.

WAR DIARY
or
INTELLIGENCE SUMMARY.
(Erase heading not required.)

Instructions regarding War Diaries and Intelligence Summaries are contained in F. S. Regs., Part II. and the Staff Manual respectively. Title pages will be prepared in manuscript.

Place	Date	Hour	Summary of Events and Information	Remarks and references to Appendices
MARGATE	25/4/18		The following draft reported	
				Sgts. Cpls. L/Cpls. Ptes. Total
			35th N.F. — 12 20 248 286
			5th R.F. — 1 3 31 35
			4th Nor. + Derby. — — 1 14 15
			52nd N.F. — — — 1 1
			4th Lincs — — — 2 2
			3701 Leicester — — — 2 2
			52nd Leicester — — — 1 1
			Total 342
			The following officers reported 2/Lieuts A.V. Bueno, A.P. McInnes, A.L. Kemp, C.B. Quantrill, T. Hyndman, J.S. Milne, & all from 1st R.G. Battn K.O.Y.L.I. Authority W.O. 66 939 M.S.I.R. 23. 2/Lieuts E.W. Bentley and G. Tricketts from 3rd D.L.I.	
	26/4/18		The following officers reported for duty. Major W.J. Hunt 7th Res. Household, Major F. Thomson North Staffs. Received command 7 th Battalion. Capt R.C. Wright 3rd Lincoln. The following drafts also arrived From 3rd S. Staffs 1 L/cpl & 13 men. 1 N.E. 14. 3rd North + Derby. 1 cpl & 10 men. N.C.E. 11. 3rd Leicester 1 cpl & 2 men Total 5. 4th N.F. 1 man. Grand Total 29. 9 a.m.	
	27/4/18		The following drafts arrived	
			s/c cpls L/C men Total
			from 35th N.F. — — 2 12 14
			5th R.F. 1 1 1 14 17
			3rd Leicester — — 1 4 5
			52nd Leicester — — — 2 2
			38
			(over)

WAR DIARY
or
INTELLIGENCE SUMMARY
(Erase heading not required.)

Army Form C. 2118.

Place	Date	Hour	Summary of Events and Information	Remarks and references to Appendices
MARGATE	2/4/18 Contd.		Capt B N Pigott 3rd Northants reported. W.D. mens 937 M.S.I.R. dated 27/4/18 received. This states the following officers of 36 Bt. N.F. will proceed overseas with the 36th. (G) Bath N.F. Capt Kaye Smeaton, Hon Capt & Q.M. S.N. Thompson, Capt B de S. Kirby, Lieut R.A. Tolminson, Lieut B.M. Tain, 2/Lieut G.N. Smith, 2/Lieut H.J. Watkins, 2/Lieut M.C. Fleming, 2/Lieut F.J. Clutterbuck, 2/Lieut L.M. Reid	pm.
MARGATE	29/4/18		Capt W.M. Langdon R.A.M.C. reports as M.O.	pm.
MARGATE	30/4/18		2/Lieut J.L. Bradley 3rd Lancashire Fusiliers reports.	pm.
MARGATE	May 3rd.		The following officers reported - all from 1st K.O.Y.L.I. Lieut J. Robinson, Lieut A.S. Dixon Lieut of Capt R.S. Haddow, 2/Lieuts A.W. Tempest, R. Stewart, E.M. Benjamin and J.B. Kitson. The following arrived from 1st K.O.Y.L.I. 2 Sergts 2 Corpls 1 L/Corps & 45 men Total 50.	pm.
MARGATE	4/5/18		During the last few days the battalion was organised in accordance with 121/FRANCE/2044 (M.S.2.1.) were instructions from 222nd Infand Bgde MARGATE. All men were full both medics SB's and P.T. Gas. All who has not been medical within last 12 months be seen done.	
"	6/5/18		Inspection of the Battalion at 3 pm by Brig Genl Glasse commanding 222nd Infd Bgde MARGATE	pm.

WAR DIARY or INTELLIGENCE SUMMARY

Army Form C. 2118.

Place	Date	Hour	Summary of Events and Information	Remarks and references to Appendices
CALAIS	7/5/18		Regt Hqrs & Battalion entraining MARGATE SANDS Station, Kent. at 2.35am. Left Rly at 3.5 am. Arrived DOVER about 4.35 am. Rested on No 3 Rest Camp till 9.30 am. Embarked on ONWARD. VILLE DE LIEGE and STAD ANTWERPEN at 11.30 am. Arrived CALAIS 1.15pm. Marched to No 6 Lens Camp (Bat.). Strength 3 Bats. arrived "arms" in CALAIS about 30 Officers and 1001 other ranks. In addition to above Transport Section & Transport left MARGATE 3am. Detrained at SOUTHAMPTON Strength 1 Officer and 50 other ranks. 1 Machine Cart, 1 Officer Mess Cart, 2 Water Carts, 10 G.S. Limbers, 4 Travelling Kitchens, and 53 animals arrived CALAIS.	
"	8/5/18		Whole Batt. (less Transport Section as yet joined 4) marched to BEAUMARAIS & remain gas instruction & have SBR's tested by passing through lacrymatory gas.	
"	9/5/18		1st Reinforcements consisting of Capt F.C. Wright, 2 Lieut F.C. Dudley and 100 O.R. left at 1.30 pm to entrain at FONTOINETTES Station for ETAPLES.	
BAILLEUL-LEZ-PERNES Sheet 36 B. A 21 d.3.2.	10/5/18		Left CALAIS. Entrained FONTOINETTES Station 11.56 am. Transport Section joining up at station. Total strength entraining 29 Officers 945 O.R. 53 animals 10 G.S. Lbrs, 4 Field Kitchens, 2 Water Carts, 1 Officers Mess Cart, 1 Machine Cart. Following rations were drawn at Station 1 hair Ration, 1 Reserve Ration. Arrived CALLON-RICOURT Station (E10.d.51.36b) 4.45 pm. Detrained. Left Railway Station 6 pm. 1 Coy Billeting Officer had been sent ahead. BAILLEUL LEZ PERNES reached 8.30 pm. All Billeted by 9.30.	
"	11/5/18		Resting. Following message received: "36 N.F killed enjoyed 10-11 and 11-12 at 9 pm. (Div.)	

WAR DIARY or INTELLIGENCE SUMMARY

Army Form C. 2118.

Place	Date	Hour	Summary of Events and Information	Remarks and references to Appendices
	12/5/18 contd.		BAILLEUL LES PERNES area. They were on 1:40,000 sheet are supplied herewith. LENS 20 HAZEBROUCK 10; 36a.b.; 36.L.b." Signed E.P. HARGRAVE Capt. for Brig Gen DA & QMG X Corps.	
ST LEONARD. I6a central.	14/5/18		Battalion parades for take to C 30 c Central. Two Officers sent ahead, to make arrangements re Company ground. One had motorbike to return to C.S.C. 2.3.6 act as guide. Head of battalion passed BAILLEUL LES PERNES Church Gam Route in a column with intructions received from HQ 59th DIVISION viz. FERFAY, CAUCHY - a la TOUR, AUCHEL. Dinners were eaten on line of march. The Company ground which was found to be I.6.c Central and not as previously notified was reached 1.30 pm. Rest of day spent in putting up tents. Digging Lieutenant the 8pm.	
"	13/5/18		Spent in reorganising the battalion. 144 partially trained Lewis gunners were rebated from the companies to training reserves. Four very important tasks. R.E. Officers reports (MAJOR REID). C.O. Adjt & Company Commanders were shown the sector of the B.B. Line which the Batt. were to dig. Sector commences at ST LEONARD I.6a Central (Sap) and runs to I.7.d 1.0 (right). On our left the 11/01 Royal Scots F. will dig & our own right a D.C.I. battalion.	
"	14/5/18		Digging Hereafter commenced. Day's task. Whole area 1 foot depth. No. 8. digging party 12 Officers & 634 other ranks. 1 RE Officer & 6 or subalterns the work. Four Company Commanders. Captains BARBER, BOND, WHEATTAN and COOK. Also Hon. Lieut & Q.M. KEERY from 2/5 th. SHERWOOD FORESTERS reports for duty. They will be accomodated and rations by this unit and will act as adviser to the present C.C. 5pm	

D.D. & L., London, E.C.
(A.10266) Wt W.5300/P713 750,000 2/18 Sch. 82 Forms/C2118/16

WAR DIARY
or
INTELLIGENCE SUMMARY.

(Erase heading not required.)

Army Form C. 2118.

Place	Date	Hour	Summary of Events and Information	Remarks and references to Appendices
I 6 a central	15/5/18		Continued digging. Strength 9 /officers 12 /NCOs + 630 o.r from lower half seven serpens to offrs of 2 /R.E. Coys.	form.
"	16/5/18		Continued digging. Strength as yesterday	form.
"	17/5/18		Continued digging. Commenced musketry range at I 6 a central.	form.
"	18/5/18		Continued digging 7:30am – 11:30am 4pm – 6pm Hostile Shelling; about a dozen shells 9 large calibre (H.E) fell in or near camp. Casualties killed 1. wounded 1. (above) Horse wounded 1. (alipa)	form.
"	19/5/18		Letter from 178th Infantry Bgde dated 18/5/18. "The front to be held in case of enemy attack will be as follows: – 362d. G.6 Balln N.F. from OURTON – BRUAY Road exclusive to CALONNE RICOUART – MARLES les MINES Road exclusive. Sheet 36 B." Continued digging.	form.
I 6 a central	20/5/18		Continued digging. Commenced moving camp by companies. A Company moved to new camping ground at I 12 a 7.2 Sheet 36 B. Site selected by the Commandant AUCHEL. D company moves to I 6 c central.	form.
"	21/5/18		Continued trench digging. B and C companies moved to new camping ground at I 12 a. Sheet 36 B.	form.
BOIS DES RIETZ I 12 a 4.1.	22/5/18		Battn HQ moved to I 12 a 4.1. Continued trench digging – pits in front of trenches for lower wire.	form.
"	23/5/18		Trench digging	form.
"	24/5/18		Trench digging	form.
"	25/5/18		Trench digging	form.

WAR DIARY or INTELLIGENCE SUMMARY

Army Form C. 2118.

Place	Date	Hour	Summary of Events and Information	Remarks and references to Appendices
BOIS DES RIETZ	26/5/18		Continued trench digging. Commander drew Second letter received from H.Q. 178th Brigade 157/13 G. "The 2Bn (G.G) Bn CHESHIRE Reg. has joined the Brigade. The Brigade frontage for the purposes of defence in case of a successful enemy attack will be divided as follows. 36th (C.G) Battn N.F - From DIEVAL - BRUAY Road inclusive to junction of communication trench and foot line about I6 d 8 2 -" Sept Peres Division for Regt. (19th Division) reports for 1 weeks duty.	7pm
" " "	27/5/18		Trench digging continues. Shelling of surrounding villages took place intermittently during this day.	9pm
" " "	28/5/18		Training all the morning. Visit of acting divisional commander Brig-Gen C N. James CB CMG at 11am. Surrounding villages BRUAY. LOZINGHEM and AUCHEL shelled during the day.	7pm
" " "	29/5/18		Trench digging continued.	8am
" " "	30/5/18		Hostile aeroplane hovered over camp during the night. Two bombs dropped on B Company's Lines. Diameter of craters 10 feet. No casualties. Continued trench digging	7pm
" " "	31/5/18		Continued Trench Digging	

Signed
Capt & Adjt
36th (C) Batt. N.F

CONFIDENTIAL

WAR DIARY

OF

36" Gn. Bn. Northumberland Fusiliers

FOR

JUNE 1918

WAR DIARY.

To HQ
178th Infantry Bgde

Herewith War Diary for June
in accordance with your instructions
96/15 G of 4/6/18.

J.F. Thomson Major
In the field   Commanding 36th (G) N F
30/6/18.

36TH G.G. BATTN
NORTHUMBERLAND
FUSILIERS.

NF 216

36'C.B. North'd Fusiliers **WAR DIARY** or **INTELLIGENCE SUMMARY** June 1918

Army Form C. 2118

Place	Date	Hour	Summary of Events and Information	Remarks and references to Appendices
BOIS DE RIETZ I.12.b.4.1 Sheet 44B	1/6/18		Trench digging. " " "	
"	2/6/18		" " "	
"	3/6/18		" " "	
"	4/6/18		Training till midday. HOUDAIN I.33.c. shelled early the morning from " digging. T.O. 2/Lieut A.E.BECKLEY severely wounded in head near PERNES. pm	
"	5/6/18		" Rec'd letter 56/13 G from Brigade H.Q. re issue "Defence scheme for the Brigade Sector of the 13.13 line. Ref. map'ps 36A & 44B @ The portion of the B.N. line to be held in case of Emergency has been increased Right Boundary Suize 3 to I.23 Central inclusive Left Boundary LINGHEM – MAZINGHEM Road inclusive The line will be divided as follows: (a) 36th G.G. Bn Northumberland Fusiliers Right Boundary Suize N3 to I.23 central Left Boundary Copse at C.24 a.0.0 & Tree No 3. Tactical Points 1. Ridge running NE from BOIS DE RIETZ 2. Ridge running NE through 15 and C.30. 3. Dry valley C.29 a.9.6 and slope S of un Northwards to apex inclusive. (b) 11th G.G. Bath Royal Scots Fusiliers Right boundary. Left B 3rd N.F. etc.	
"	6/6/18		East of the above tactical points are to be held by one Company deployed in depth. Battalion must keep one Company in Reserve to carry out and execute counter attack. Battalion will detail certain parties under an Officer of proceeding avenues of approach from the direction of the enemy at 36th NF. ① Road in I.7a ② Railway in I.6. ③ Cross Roads on PERNES – MARLES LES MINES Road at C.30.d.2.4 ④ Railway junction at C.24.c.6.0 All moving detachments will fight on the ground they occupy. Under no circumstances any withdrawal take place without a definite order from Brigade H.Q. Brigade H.Q. now open at CHATEAU FERFAY. Signed Brigade Major 178th Inf Brigade	

Army Form C. 2118

36th B. Northumberland Fusiliers June 1918

WAR DIARY or INTELLIGENCE SUMMARY

(Erase heading not required.)

Instructions regarding War Diaries and Intelligence Summaries are contained in F.S. Regs., Part II. and the Staff Manual respectively. Title Pages will be prepared in manuscript.

Place	Date	Hour	Summary of Events and Information	Remarks and references to Appendices
BOIS DE RIETZ Sheet 44A. I.12.b.4.1.	7/6/18		Trench Digging. Operation Order No 1. Ref map of France 1/40,000 Sheet 44.B 7/6/18 1. Bdry of Bn. line to be held by 36 N.F. in case of emergency is trenches as follows:— R. Boundary Sege No 3 BRUAY I 23 central inclusive. L " " C24.a.00 to face 3 de MARLES inclusive. 2. Intention To hold the following tactical points each by one company disposed as under a. 1 Company holding ridge running NE from BOIS DE RIETZ, disposed as follows ½ Platoon in trench from I 18 6 34 to BOIS DE RIETZ – BRUAY Road inclusive. 1 Platoon in trench from BOIS DE RIETZ – BRUAY road exclusive to trench at I 12 6 90 inc. 1 Platoon from trench at I 12 6 90 exclusive to about point I 12 d 4.3 2 Platoons (support) in trench about point I 12 d 4.3 Company HQ at I 12 d 4.3 b. 1 Company holding ridge running NE through I 5 and C 30 disposed as follows 1 Platoon in trench from I 6 c 4 8 (RIVER CLARENCE) exclusive to ST LEONARD – MARLES LES MINES road inclusive. 1 Platoon in trench from ST LEONARD – MARLES LES MINES road inclusive to about point in trench C 30 c 4 5 most inclusive 2 Platoons (support) about ST in ST LEONARD I 5 6 6 5 Coy HQ at I 5 6 6 5 c. 1 Coy holding valley C 29 a & C 29 b and slopes of spur northwards disposed as follows ½ Platoon in trench from about point C 30 c 4 5 to about entrance at C 30 c 2 8 ½ Platoon from about point C 29 b 5.0 to about C 29 b 3 3 ½ Platoon along trench on high ground N. of railway to back about C 23 d 9 5 ½ Platoon in trench from back about C 23 d 9.3 to about point C 24 c 3 8 2 Platoons (support) about C 29 a 8.5 Coy HQ about C 29 a 8.5 d. 1 Company (Batln Tactical Reserve) in sunk road about I 12 c 8 4. 3. Garrisons of posts will in no case be less than ½ platoons 4. All units & detachments will fight on ground they occupy. Owing to circumstances will any withdrawal take place without direct orders from Batln H.Q. or higher authority.	

Army Form C. 2118

WAR DIARY or INTELLIGENCE SUMMARY

(Erase heading not required.)

J6 C.A. Northumberland Fusiliers   June 1918

Instructions regarding War Diaries and Intelligence Summaries are contained in F. S. Regs., Part II. and the Staff Manual respectively. Title Pages will be prepared in manuscript.

Place	Date	Hour	Summary of Events and Information	Remarks and references to Appendices
I 12 b 4.1	7/6/18 continued	5	OC Companies will detail collecting parties each under an Officer for collecting stragglers & bodies of troops arriving & approach. They will be responsible for conducting stragglers & bodies of troops without definite orders into B.H.Q line. Guides between companies will be these tiles in order & supervision. Company tracking BOIS DE RIETZ Mark Ridge Company tracking ST LEONARD Ridge Company tracking valley C29a & C29b (a) Roads in J7a (b) Railway in I 6 (c) Cross Roads C 30 d 2.4 (d) Railway junction C 24 c 6.0	
		6	Battn S.A.A. Reserve at I 10 a 88 under R.S.M.	
		7	1st Line Transport (less the limits with Coys) parked at I 10 a 88.	
		8	Dressing Station at I 10 a 88.	
		9	2nd in Command (Major W.J. HUNT 36th N.F.) will be at BOIS DE RIETZ.	
		10	Battn HQ will be at I 4 c 6.3 to which place all reports will be sent.	
			Signed J Thomson Major Commanding 36th (GC) N.F. 7/6/18	
			Road not taken by 2nd in C Report in A.B.C &D Coys at 9pm Sept – L/Col Spencerlain 1 Copy to Brigade	9 pm 9 pm
	8/6/18		Trench Digging continued.	
	9/6/18		Manning trenches 8am to 11am. Dispositions as in Operation Orders See 7/6/18. A dozen large shells burst in AUCHEL between 9am & 10am.	pm 10 am
	10/6/18		Trench Digging	pm
	11/6/18		" "	5 pm
	12/6/18		" "	5 pm
	13/6/18		" "	8 pm
	14/6/18		" "	9 pm
	15/6/18		" " Letter 119/17 G received from 178th Infantry Bgde HQ with Div letter 437/17 G	8 pm

WAR DIARY / INTELLIGENCE SUMMARY

Army Form C. 2118.

36 I.B.
Northumberland Fusiliers
June 1918

Hour, Date, Place	Summary of Events and Information	Remarks and references to Appendices
15/6/18 continued I 12.6.41	attached. Orders from Comdr. read "The Division is to commence a period of training to fit it to take its place in a quiet sector of the line. It is hoped that about 2 months will be available" gam.	
16/6/18 H 23 c 6.6. Sheet 44 B. 9 p.m.	178th Infantry Bgde. Order No 118 received at 4.45 am. Stated inter alia "1. The 178th Infantry Bgde. (less 2nd G Bn Royal Irish Reg and 23rd GG Battn Chesh'n Reg) will move today to the TANGRY area. 2. 36th GG Battn N.F. to MAREST Rendez Cross Rds I 27 c 9.8 – Corner Rds Z 20 c 13 – Cross Rds H 20 b 9.4 – MAREST 6 Battns will Stand at 6 am. 12. The transport of the 36th GG Battn N.F. will move via CAMBLAIN-CHATELAIN." The move area commenced at 9 am. MAREST being reached at 11.45 am. 3 Companies were billeted & one fed under canvas.	
17/6/18 PRÉDEFIN 6 D 11 Hazebrouck Sheet 5a 9 p.m.	178th Brigade No 119 (Order) received at 9.30 pm 16/6/18 states "The Brigade will move tomorrow from 17th to the BOMY Training Area in accordance with attached March Table. - - 36th N.F from MAREST to PRÉDEFIN at 6.00 am via SAINS-lez-PERNES and FIEFS." The Battalion left MAREST at 6 am and arrived at PRÉDEFIN at 11.15 am. A billeting party had been sent ahead and all were billeted by 12.00	
18/6/18 PRÉDEFIN.	Companies were all day with the exception of Orderly and kit inspections. Orders from Comdr. Pamphlet 7/33 received from Bgde "Training of German Divisions" Dated 13/6/18. Stated from Comdr. "Having in view the work Red three divisions may be called on to perform, the training carried out by them in training areas should be minutious accordingly. Tanks should be devoted mainly to Musketry-Musketry, Gas Drill, Route marches, steady Drill, Bayonet & Rifle Bombing & Clean fire. No attempt should be made to practise open warfare, but officers & NCO's should be instructed in tactics on company work & map reading. Battalion should leave the area at establishment & equipment, tanks in the same status as usual	

26 G.Bn North'd Fus WAR DIARY

Army Form C. 2118.

June 1918

WAR DIARY or INTELLIGENCE SUMMARY.
(Erase heading not required.)

Hour, Date, Place	Summary of Events and Information	Remarks and references to Appendices
18/6/18 PRÉDEFIN (Continued)	On C of I. & O.O. 19/19 GHQ dated June 14th 1918 received from Bde "Organisation of the Infantry Battn." Establishment 900 Other ranks (temporarily) Each Platoon to consist of 2 rifle sections & a double L.G. section.	
19/6/18 PRÉDEFIN 9 pm	Training in accordance with above. 180 other ranks inoculations duty. Through a form of BRONCHITIS. Major Gen Sir R D WHIGHAM KCB DSO in command of Divn in pm	9 pm
20/6/18 "	Training. 146 other ranks in Hospital. 80 other sick and nursing duty.	9 pm
21/6/18 "	Training. At 11.30 am Major General Sir R D WHIGHAM K.C.B. D.S.O. inspected the Battalion at training.	8 pm
22/6/18 "	Training & Bathing arrived and as well as possible. 146 Hospital cases. 34 other sick and 51 on nursing duty.	8 pm
23/6/18 "	SUNDAY. Church Parades. 46 the continuation of training owing to sickness.	8 pm
24/6/18 "	57 Reinforcements arrived from Base (ETAPLES) Serjts 1. Corpls 3. L/Corpls 2. Men 51. Total 57	8 pm
25/6/18 "	Sent 52 or (Serjts 1 Corpls 1 L/Corpls 5 men 45) to Base, no account with exchanging countries in Bges menage A Q 40 of 24/6/18. Those 52 had been exchanges etc. B2 or B3, by the Inspector of Staff on June 14. Inspection of the Battalion at training by Lieut Gen Sir W. E. PEYTON KCB Commanding X Corps	8 pm
26/6/18 "	Training. Letter A2084/58/1 of 25/6/18 received stating that distinguishing patches will be worn by all ranks... 36th N.F. A green triangle (2 inch equilateral) worn on the outside of both sleeves the highest point being 3" below the seam of the shoulder strap.	Divisional letter
27/6/18 "	Training. Letter Q 2109/58 of 26/6/18 received from H Q Division stating that all vehicles of this unit will bear an identification marks blunt square of 10 inch side. In the right hand bottom corner will be painted in white size 2" the Cypher letter & number P.1.	8 pm
28/6/18 "	Inspection of Battalion by Brigade Commander Brig Gen T.W. Stansfeld CMG DSO	8 pm

WAR DIARY
or
INTELLIGENCE SUMMARY.
(Erase heading not required.)

Army Form C. 2118.

36 I.B.
Month June 1918.

Hour, Date, Place		Summary of Events and Information	Remarks and references to Appendices
29/6/18 TRÉDEFIN.	7pm	Letter 510/7 dated 28/6/18 received from Brigade stating that the following postings have been ordered by A.G. G.H.Q. 10 Officers of the Northumberland Fusrs to join 36th G. Battn. N.F. 2 Captains to be endorsed. Authority A.G/2158/3853 (o) dated 27/6/18 -	mem.
30/6/18	9pm	Ten Officers as named on 29/6/18 reports about 7h45 29/6/18. Capt R.R. ROBERTSON Capt E.W. MOYES. 2/Lieut J.L. PIGGOTT 2/Lieut J.A. TAYLOR 2/Lieut J. HENDRY 2/Lieut J.O. SCOTT 2/Lieut N.E. HAZLEDINE 2/Lieut A.C. McWILLIAM 2/Lieut F. WILLIAMSON 2/Lieut J.W. LACEY	8pm

ORIGINAL.

WAR DIARY

36TH BN NORTHD FUSILIERS.

JULY 1918

26" Northumberland Fus

WAR DIARY
or
INTELLIGENCE SUMMARY.
(Erase heading not required.)

Army Form C. 2118.

Instructions regarding War Diaries and Intelligence Summaries are contained in F.S. Regs., Part II. and the Staff Manual respectively. Title pages will be prepared in manuscript.

Hour, Date, Place	Summary of Events and Information	Remarks and references to Appendices
9 pm 1/7/18 TRÉPEIN Sheet 44C F.22.d.5.1.	Training.	Serene.
9 pm 2/7/18 "	Training	Fair
9 pm 3/7/18 "	Training	Fair
9 pm 4/7/18 "	Route March in morning. At 5.15 pm practice 'emergency move'. Bollobie (fighting strength) went 1st Line transport ready to move 6.5 minutes after receiving the order.	Fair
9 pm 5/7/18 "	Training.	Fair
9 pm 6/7/18 "	Proceeded to DELETTE (HAZEBROUCK 5a S G 72) to practise a trench relief	Fair
9 pm 7/7/18 "	Back from DELETTE at 2.30 pm	Fair
9 pm 8/7/18 "	Training	Fair
9 pm 9/7/18 "	Training	Fair
9 pm 10/7/18 "	Training & Route march.	Fair
9 pm 11/7/18 "	Training	Fair
9 pm 12/7/18 "	Training	Fair
9 pm 13/7/18 "	Training. Inspection at 5 pm by Gen Sir H.S. Horne K.C.B. K.C.M.G. Commanding 1st Army. Capt A W Prisott returned T.S. Wilson sent to Base Church parade. [to rest on production]	Fair
9 pm 14/7/18 "	Training. C.O. left at 10 am for 4 days duty in trenches.	Fair
9 pm 15/7/18 "	Training	Fair
9 pm 16/7/18 "	Training	Fair
9 pm 17/7/18 "	Route march.	Fair
9 pm 18/7/18 "	Tactical Scheme	Fair
9 pm 19/7/18 "	Training.	Serene.

Army Form C. 2118.

WAR DIARY
or
INTELLIGENCE SUMMARY.
(Erase heading not required.)

Instructions regarding War Diaries and Intelligence Summaries are contained in F.S. Regs., Part II. and the Staff Manual respectively. Title pages will be prepared in manuscript.

Hour, Date, Place	Summary of Events and Information	Remarks and references to Appendices
9pm 20/7/18 PREDEFIN Sheet 44 C F22 d.5.1.	2 Companies A and B from a raid to Hofmund Line trenches at FESTUBERT (Royal Sussex Regt). Strength 1 party 300 all ranks. Embussed at PREDEFIN Church at 4pm. Detrained at F28&26 Sheet 44.15 on SAILLY-LA-BOURSE — ANNEQUIN Road at 9.15pm.	9pm
9pm 21/7/18.	2 Companies in trenches as above.	9pm
9pm 22/7/18	2 Companies arrives from raid to trenches at 7.30pm. 2 at PREDEFIN	9pm
9pm 23/7/18 Sheet 51 C. P.18.d GOUY EN ARTOIS	Bgde Order No 122 dated 23/7/18 received at 9.45pm states that the Bgde (less 25th KRR) would move 23/7/18 to the BARLY area; the 25th KRR remain back to move on July 25th. 1st line transport would go ahead. Units arranged in lorries & buses. Starting point LIId 3.5 (Sheet 44 C) Detraining point Pro C 9.1. (Sheet 57 C) on BARLY-FOSSEUX Road. The unit then marched to its billets at GOUY. Interior economy and rest. The Division has commenced to relieve the 3rd Canadian Division. Whew relief is complete the 176 Infantry Bgde will be in the line with HQ at BLAIRVILLE QUARRY. The 177 & 13gth Bgdes with HQ at BRETENCOURT CHATEAU & the 178th Bgde with HQ at BARLY Chateau. Reconnoitring parties (consisting 1 Co. Adjt, Intelligence Off, Signal Officer & 4 Company Commanders & 8 Subalterns from each Battalion) reports at HQ 7th Canadian Infantry Bgde at 10 am to reconnoitre the PURPLE System. Men by lorry from GOUY.	9pm Sheet 51 C
9pm 24/7/18. GOUY.		
9pm 25/7/18. GOUY.	Training as far as cramped facilities would allow.	9pm
9pm 26/7/18 "	Training	9pm
9pm 27/7/18 "	"	9pm
9pm 28/7/18 "	Church Parade - Rest.	9pm
9pm 29/7/18 "	Training. Practice of Trench Relief.	9pm

Army Form C. 2118.

36th Northumberland Fusiliers

WAR DIARY
or
INTELLIGENCE SUMMARY.
(Erase heading not required.)

Instructions regarding War Diaries and Intelligence Summaries are contained in F. S. Regs., Part II. and the Staff Manual respectively. Title pages will be prepared in manuscript.

Hour, Date, Place	Summary of Events and Information	Remarks and references to Appendices
9 am. 30/7/18. GOUY Sheet 57C D.2.d.	G.O.C. 59th Division inspected the Battalion at 11.30 am. at P.24.d.59. G.O.C. 178th Brigade lectured to Officers of Brigade at 3.30 pm. on "Trench Entrishn." at Brigade Headquarters, BARLY.	Init.
9 am. 31/7/18 "	Training	Init.

J.F. Thurston
Lt Colonel Comdg.
36th Bn. Northumberland Fusiliers

CONFIDENTIAL.

WAR DIARY

36th NORTHUMBERLAND FUS.

FOR

AUGUST, 1918.

Army Form C. 2118.

36 Northumberland Fusiliers

WAR DIARY
INTELLIGENCE SUMMARY.

August 1918.

Place	Date	Hour	Summary of Events and Information	Remarks and references to Appendices
GOUY-EN-ARTOIS. P.19.C. Sheet 51.C	1/8/18	9 pm	Training. Inspection by Lieut General Sir Aylmer Haldane, K.C.B, D.S.O, Commanding VI Corps. 178th Infty. Brigade order No. 123 dated 31st July, 1918, received with reference to the relief of 178th. Brigade by the 176th. Brigade (See appendix A.)	App.
			Advance party consisting of 4 Company Commanders, their batmen, 2 runners, 12 Observers and Intelligence Officer proceeded to the trenches to take over from 17th. Royal Sussex Regt. Commanding Officer and Adjutant proceeded to make forward their reconnaissance, returning the same night.	
"	2/8/18	9 pm	Battalion entrained at BAVINCOURT (P.28.a.8.2) at 6-30 p.m and detrained at Manchester Arch (M.21.c.) at 9.45 p.m. Guides from 17th. Bn. R. Sussex Regt. led the various Companies into their positions in the trenches. Owing to shell fire, inclement weather and darkness, the relief was delayed, owing to the Guides missing their way. Relief was reported complete at 6.30 am 3.8.18. One casualty – killed by T.M. Shell. Weather very wet.	kind
MERCATEL SWITCH SUPPORT M.H.a.2.4. Sh.51.B. S.W.	3.8.18	9	The Battalions front extends from S.13.d.1.9 (Road inclusive) to M.36.B.O.O. Two Companies in the Line, 2 in Support. The Battns. front is divided into 2 Sectors, Right and Left. A Company hold the Right. B. Coy the Left. with C. & D. Companies in Support respectively on our Right next to the Sussex Division on our left a Bn of the Essex Regt. On the left of our Brigade 2 extended trenches "The BRICK FIELDS" S.2 and S.3. and the "CHAT MAIRES" S.27 are held by the 116. R. Scots Fusiliers. a.o. a Patrol by left Coy. Investigated positions.	kind

WAR DIARY
INTELLIGENCE SUMMARY

36th M.G. Bn Aux? Army Form C. 2118.

August 1918

Place	Date	Hour	Summary of Events and Information	Remarks and references to Appendices
MERCATEL SWITCH SUPT B10.a.2.4 Sh51.b.6.SW	4.8.18	9 p.m.	On night of 3rd 2 ku? patrols of 1 officer and 7 other Ranks left our line at 10.30 am to patrol our wire and find out gaps, also to locate positions of M.G.s & L.T.M.S. in no mans land. Patrols returned at 12.30. Reporting gaps but not the locations of M.Gs or L.T.MS each ku?	ku?
"	5.8.18	9 p.m.	On night of 4th 2 patrols of 1 officer and 7 O.R. each left our line at 11 p.m. to locate positions of M G.s & L.T. Ms in Nomans land with a view to previous action. Patrols reported M.G. posts in S.12.a.3.7. and a snipers post at S.6.c.7.5. A and B. Coys in front line were relieved by C. and D. Coys. Very wet night.	ku?
"			Instructions from 178th Bde. were received on 4th August for patrols to go out on night of 5/6 & 6/7th to ascertain (a) Enemy position and approximate strength of L.M.G. post at approximately S.12.a.8.8. (b) To reconnoitre No mans land in S.6.a where recent enemy trenches had been reported. No news of recent occupation.	ku?
"	6.8.18	9 p.m.	On night of 5th. Patrol of 1 officer & 4 Bn Scouts left O.T. at S.6.A.1.9 east, and to report any signs of recent occupation. and patrolled S.6.a. found trenches, but no signs of recent occupation. Another patrol left Observation Trench at S.12.a.2.8. patrolled wire but could find no indicates gaps, re-entered trench & crossed River COJEUL leaving O.T. again at S.12.a.4.5. Patrolled wire again but was unsuccessful in finding any gap, the fact that very bad weather and long grass obscured the wire made the reconnaissance very difficult	

WAR DIARY **INTELLIGENCE SUMMARY**

36 North'd Fusiliers Army Form C. 2118

August 1918

Place	Date	Hour	Summary of Events and Information	Remarks and references to Appendices
MERCATEL SWITCH SUPPORT	7.8.18	9 p.m.	No patrols left our lines on night of 6th inst. Weather much better. Trenches are now beginning to dry.	Initp.
"	8.8.18	9 p.m.	2 Patrols of 1 Officer and 7 O.R. each left to locate Snipers & M.G. posts in No man's land. No. 1 Patrol left our line at 10.30 p.m. at S.6.6.15.20. - Two shots fired from this locality like a Snipers post at S.6.a.05.70. Reported what appears from observation of discerning Very lights it would appear that the enemy line is some considerable distance from the line of this patrol. No. 2 Patrol left our line at 10.30 p.m. and returned at 12.35 a.m. No enemy sniper fired on this patrol & no snipers posts nor M.G. posts were located. Visibility poor owing to heavy mist.	keep
"	9.8.18	9 p.m.	Patrols left our lines last night to reconnoitre. No news heard entire enemy is discerned and to obtain prisoners or identifications. No enemy were encountered & from the appearance of last encroachean grass it would appear that no patrols have been beyond our second line except for some hour. Very lights show the enemy line lithe at least 600 x from our forward position. No 2 Patrol proceeded N.E. via LONG ALLEY for about 1500 x towards HENIN. No recent signs of enemy occupation was discovered & no opposition of any sort was met with. Both patrols returned safely. Weather good.	Initp.

WAR DIARY or INTELLIGENCE SUMMARY

Army Form C. 2118

36 North Fusiliers

August 1918

Place	Date	Hour	Summary of Events and Information	Remarks and references to Appendices
1 BRICKFIELDS S.2.b.52.	10.8.18	9 p.m.	Battalion is to be relieved in the Outpost System on night of 10/11 August, by 11th. R.S.F. A Coy. relieved by C. Coy. Royal Scots. Fusiliers B " " D " " C " " A " " D " " B " " When relieved Companies will be led to their positions in BRICKFIELDS. B Coy commenced relief at 2.30 p.m. and was completed by 4.30 p.m. A " " " 4.30 " " " " 6.30 " B " " " 6.30 p.m. and opened at S.2.b.5.2 (BRICKFIELDS) Battn. H.Q. closed at M.4.a.2.4. 6.30 p.m. and opened at S.2.b.5.2 (BRICKFIELDS) at 6.30 p.m. Weather very good. Casualties Nil.	Nil.
"	11.8.18	9 p.m.	At 9.30 p.m. 10.8.18 Two Platoons of A. Coy + two Platoons B Coy of 11th. R.S.F. were met at S.3.b. 40.35 by guides of this Bttn and conducted to their positions in Front line where they relieved the forward Platoons of C. + D. Coy. At 10:30 p.m. the remaining two platoons of A. + B. Coys R.S.F. were met by guides at S.3.b. 40.35 and conducted to their positions in Seuik Road S.5.a. 2.3 where they relieved the support platoons of C. + D. Coy. 38th. N.F. Relief of C. + D. Coy 36th N.F. by A + B. Coys 11th. R.S.F. was completed by 2 a.m. Weather excellent. Casualties Nil.	Nil.

WAR DIARY 36 North'd Fusiliers Army Form C. 2118.

or

INTELLIGENCE SUMMARY.

(Erase heading not required.)

August 1918.

Place	Date	Hour	Summary of Events and Information	Remarks and references to Appendices
BRICKFIELDS	12/8/18	9 pm	In Reserve. Casualties 1. 11-8-18. G.S.W. arm. Weather excellent.	Lieut R. PMn.
BRICKFIELDS	13/8/18	"	Quiet day	PMn
BELLACOURT Sheet 51C SE R.31	14/8/18	9 pm	Relieved in BRICKFIELDS by 13th West Ridings. Relief 10pm to 1pm am Successful. Battalion on relief marched to BELLACOURT. All safely billeted by 4 am 14/8/18. Rest till 12 noon. Remainder of day cleaning up & bathing.	9 am PMn
Ditto	15/8/18	9 pm	Training commenced. Total casualties whilst in trenches 2/3rd to 13/14th. Killed 1 Wounded 2.	8 pm PMn
Ditto	16/8/18	9 pm	Training	9 pm PMn
Ditto	17/8/18	4 pm	Training - morning	9 pm PMn
BARLY P.15. Sheet 51C SE P.15 c 9.5.7.5.	18/8/18	9 pm	Battalion marches last night starting at 5 pm from BELLACOURT to BARLY. Marching out Strength of Battalion 28 officers 770 other ranks.	9 am PMn Sgt 796.
Ditto	20/8/18	9 pm	Training	9 pm PMn
Sheet 51C SE X 4d 4.6	21/8/18	12 midnight	Sudden orders received at 10 am to 'STAND TO' preparatory to move. Message received at 1:50 pm to entrain at BARLY at 2:30 pm. Travelled by lorry to BLAIRVILLE X.4. Bivouacs till dusk. Guides from 1st Battn Welsh Guards reports 8:15 pm. Relieved 1st Battn Welsh Guards. Relief complete 11:30 pm.	9 pm PMn
X 4d 4.6	22/8/18	9 pm	Disposition of Battn A Company as permanent battalion on the station in Sunken in the Support Line of entrance at S.9.b and d. Sheet 51B. SW. B and C companies as permanent battalion on Hill 115 on the	

WAR DIARY or INTELLIGENCE SUMMARY.

Army Form C. 2118.

36th North Irish Horse

August 1918

Place	Date	Hour	Summary of Events and Information	Remarks and references to Appendices
SAULTY. Long 11 4 G centrals	23rd	11 pm	Purple Line B at 87.b Sheet 51.b SW. and X.12.c 51.c SE C at S.1.b and 8.2.c Sheet 51.b SW. D at X.4.b and d Sheet 51.c SE with its base position on Hues 115. D Company in reserve at X.4.6 and d Sheet 51.c SE with its base position on Hues 115.	8 p.m.
			Message received from Major N.G. at 9.30 pm stating that Battalion would entrain at 1 am to BRETENCOURT. Battalion arrived BRETENCOURT at 3.30. Bivouaced for night in fields. Order No 128 (12th Infantry Bgde) received at 8 am stating that Battalion was to be prepared to move to SAULTY on receipt 7 orders; and that 59th Division was moving in by Takent Train to WAIL area on 24th. Telegram received ordering march from BRETENCOURT to SAULTY. March 5pm to 8.30 pm. Bivouac for night in fields outside station.	pm
MANQUEVILLE Sheet 36a Solden 6 U.3.6.	24.	11 pm	59th Division Administration Instruction No 29 received 12 midnight 23rd stating (inter alia) that battalion would entrain at SAULTY station at 11.42 am 24th for WAIL area. Detrained at BERGUETTE about 8 pm; marched from thence to MANQUEVILLE. Battalion billeted in village.	pm
Ditto	25.	9 pm	Day spent in bathing and interior economy. Buggage which had been sent to WAIL area arrives during afternoon.	pm
Ditto	26.	9 pm	Reconnaissance party of 7 officers visited ROBECQ to took over sector area 3 hours system there.	pm
ROBECQ P.23 & S.2 Sheet 36a Edition 6	27.	9 pm	Relieved 11th S.L.I. Light MANQUEVILLE in 2 convoys at 2.30 and 4.30 pm. Relay company by 7.30 pm. Disposition 3 companies in letter in ROBECQ and 1 in trenches at Q.19.6.	pm
Ditto	28	9 pm	Day spent in salvage hunts, ordinations economy.	pm J.H.

D. D. & L., London, E.C.
(A10056) Wt.W5300/P713 750,000 2/18 Sch. 22 Forms/C2118/16

WAR DIARY
INTELLIGENCE SUMMARY

36 North'd Fusiliers   Army Form C. 2118.

August 1918

Place	Date	Hour	Summary of Events and Information	Remarks and references to Appendices
ROBECQ	29	9 p.m.	Three Coys Training.	3396 appx
Ditto.	30	9 p.m.	Three Coys training.	
Sheet 36A Q.6.A.40.20.	31	9 p.m.	The following wire telegram received from 178 Infantry Brigade at 2.20pm. "178 Infantry Bde will move forward to the line LA CROIX MARMEUSE — EPINETTE — MEURILLON new 36th Northumberland Fus will harrow a long ABBY ROAD in squares R.13 and R.20 new 13th West Ridings Regt on the EPINETTE — MEURILLON new EPINETTE inclusive to left battalion new 11th Royal Scots Regt will remain in brigade reserve and will bivouac in squares Q.18A and Q.12C new First Line transport can be taken of Quartermasters stores and packs should be left in present area new On reaching destination 36th Northumberland Fusiliers and 13th West Ridings will reconnoitre a suitable line to be held in case of emergency new acknowledge new 178 Infantry Bde will close at LA HAYE at 6 p.m. and open at CALONNE P.4.c.24. on arrival new Antaran addressed Bn's and T.M.B. repeated 59th Division app" Message ends. Battn. left ROBECQ 5.15 p.m. and arrived at ABBY Road 7.45 p.m.	

WAR DIARY
or
INTELLIGENCE SUMMARY

Army Form C. 2118.

36 North Fusiliers

August 1918

Place	Date	Hour	Summary of Events and Information	Remarks and references to Appendices
	31/8	9 am cont	Disposition of Battalion :— Two Coys holding line of posts 40ᵡ W of ABBYₐₙₑ in squares R.13 and two Coys in support along road in squares Q.16d, Q.18c, Q.24a, Q.24c.	396.
			In the field 31/8/18	
			J.F.Thomson. Lieut Col. Commanding 36.N.F.	

Confidential

War Diary

of

36 Bn. Northumberland Fusiliers.

September 1918.

Confidential

WAR DIARY

36TH BATTN.,
NORTHUMBERLAND
FUSILIERS.

No. NF 836

To HQ
  178th Infantry Brigade.

Herewith War Diary (Original)
for month ending Sept 30th.

30/9/18
                J.F. Thomson
                    Lt Col
                Cdg 36th N.F.

WAR DIARY
or
INTELLIGENCE SUMMARY.
(Erase heading not required.)

Army Form C. 2118.

Place	Date	Hour	Summary of Events and Information	Remarks and references to Appendices
Sheet 36a Q.12.4.b.20	Sept 1st	9 pm	3rd Battn in Divisional reserve.	
Sheet 36a R.15.d.40.95.	2/9/16	9 pm	178th Infantry Brigade order No 130 received 2.30 p.m., at stations which advanced. "General Brigade will relieve 177 Infantry Bde on the Advanced Brigade today September 2nd as follows:— 1. The 179 Northumberland Fusiliers will relieve 2/6 D.L.I. The Right Front Battalion. 2. The 36th The 13th West Riding Regt will relieve 11th Somerset L.I. the Left Front Battalion. The 178 L.T.M.B. will relieve the 177 L.T.M.B. 3. The 11th T.R.S.F. will be in Support at Rue Delanney in R.20.6. 4. Units will move by march route. 10. Brigade Headquarters will close at Q.4.c.4.2. and reopen at R.9.c.2.7 on arrival. The Battn started at 4 pm. and arrived at new Battn H.Q. at 4.42 pm. Disposition of Battn:— Battn H.Q. at R.15.d.40.95. Sheet 36a. Three Coys holding new frontage through R.17.a, R.17.6, R.17.c, R.18.c, R.24.a and Ravel from R.24.a.0.3. to R.24.a.0.0. now one Coy in Support at R.22.6, all map references Sheet 36a.	2/6

Army Form C. 2118.

WAR DIARY
or
INTELLIGENCE SUMMARY.
(Erase heading not required.)

Place	Date	Hour	Summary of Events and Information	Remarks and references to Appendices
R.18.c.25,20	3/9/18	9 A.M.	The 178 Infantry Brigade orders No.131 dated 18 noon 2/9/18, received 1 A.M. 3/9/18 state	

"1. The 19th Division will attack Trescault S-Vaast and Croix Barbée tomorrow morning September 3rd. 36th Northumberland Fus. will co-operate by attacking at the same time and capturing Eaton, Harrow, and Charterhouse Posts.
2nd Battn. Wilts Regt. will be on the right of the 36th No.Fus.

"2. The attack will be carried out in two courses:-
    First objective Eaton Post Locality.
    Second objective Harrow and Charterhouse Localities.

"The rate of advance will be 100/m. in two minutes.

"3. The following Artillery will assist the Infantry in the attack:-

1-18 pdr. battery on Harrow, zero to zero plus 30
1-18 pdr. battery on M19.d.80,65, zero to zero plus 10.
Lift on to Harrow Post zero plus 10 & remain till zero plus 30.
1-18 pdr. battery on Clifton Central zero to zero plus 30
1-4.5 How. battery on Charterhouse zero to zero plus 12, then lift to protective barrage

1-4.5 battery on Houses in M.14.d zero to zero plus 12 then join Protective barrage.

WAR DIARY
or
INTELLIGENCE SUMMARY.

Army Form C. 2118.

Place	Date	Hour	Summary of Events and Information	Remarks and references to Appendices
R.20.c.2.5.	3/9/18	9 p.m.	"Rate of fire = 18 rounds per gun per minute." " " - 4.5 Hows 3 rounds per gun per minute. "Heavy Arty will engage points EAST of final objective. (Details on Appdx.) 4. Two guns 178th L.T.M.B. will report to each of the front line battalions immediately on receipt of these orders. "6. After capture of the posts mentioned in para 1. strong fighting patrols will be sent out by both front line battalions to keep in touch with "the enemy, working on the objective ESTAIRES - LA BASSEE Road. "If it is found that the attack on the above posts from the WEST is unsuccessful then the attacking troops must at once arrange and capture these posts from the SOUTH. It is absolutely essential that touch should be gained at once with the 19th Division and that our troops move forward with the 19th Division and not ZERO. "Rather than having any gap at all be between these men as a on a flanking "troops should therefor the 19th Division. 6. The attack is being covered by a number of our aeroplanes flying low, and attacking the enemy with machine gun fire. a Contact Aeroplane will call on the Klaxon Horn 7AM, 1PM and 7PM. 7 Listen Posts will be established with 19 Division M.20.c 9.0 and M.20.d 5.0.	

Army Form C. 2118.

WAR DIARY
or
INTELLIGENCE SUMMARY.
(Erase heading not required.)

Place	Date	Hour	Summary of Events and Information	Remarks and references to Appendices
R.18.c.25.20.	3/9/18	9 p.m.	"8." Battle. orders synchronised at 9p.m. and 2a.m.	
		"9." "ZERO" hour will be 5.30 a.m. September 3rd." Order ends.	
			The Batt. advanced as ordered in the following manner.	
		A. Coy. 5.30 am.	Advanced on 1000ˣ front. Nos. 1, 3rd 4 Platoons in front line and No. 2 Platoon and Coy. H.Q. in close support. Met Machine gun opposition at CHARTERHOUSE and ETON POSTS, drove out M.G. team from CHARTERHOUSE.	
		6.a.m.	Reached first objective including ETON POST.	
		6.45 am	Reached final objective – LA BASSÉE – ESTAIRES ROAD at PONT DU HEM Cross Road. Enemy running about 800ˣ North. One M.G. captured at PONT DU HEM Cross Roads by No.4 Platoon. 2 of the gunners were captured and the remainder of the team killed.	
		7.15 am	Established line East of LA BASSÉE Road with 3 Platoons and one platoon in close support.	
		8.30 am.	Fighting patrols reported ground clear of enemy to HAILEYBURY ROAD Captured 2 M.Gs. which had been heavily abandoned by the enemy.	
		8.0 pm.	Relieved by C. Coy. and retired to HARROW POST in support to B. Coy.	
		B. Coy. at 5.30 a.m.	with the exception of No.5 Platoon took up A. Coy position at ROUT DEVILLE POST when A. Coy advanced.	
		10 am.	Advanced to support A. Coy. taking up positions in M. 30. C and d.	
		6 p.m.	moved forward & established outpost line from M. 22 d. 15.15 to M. 15. d. 70.10.	Lieut
		C. Coy at 10.30 am.	advanced from their position at MANOR LANE (R.18 a) for about 1500ˣ taking up a forward position on LA BASSÉE Road in M.14. b.	

Army Form C. 2118.

WAR DIARY
or
INTELLIGENCE SUMMARY.
(Erase heading not required.)

Place	Date	Hour	Summary of Events and Information	Remarks and references to Appendices
R.18.c.25.20.	3/9/18	9 pm	C. Coy at 4.45 pm. D. Coy passed through C. Coy taking up a forward position on HAILEYBURY ROAD. C. Coy in support to D. Coy.	
			D. Coy at 6.30 am. sent forward a patrol from their front line (R.17.a.5.9, to R.17.a.4.8) to report whether it was possible to occupy the Road Junction at R.17.c.5.9.	
		8.15 am	Post pushed forward to R.17.c.5.9.	
		9.0 am	Patrol reported CLIFTON NORTH POST clear of enemy. Machine Gun active about R.12.o.7.2.	
		10.0 am	After reconnaissance by Coy. Cdr. Coy moved forward to line CLIFTON NORTH POST to CLIFTON SOUTH POST.	
		11.30 am	Patrol returned reporting no enemy, except a solitary sniper somewhere W. of LA BASSEE Road.	
		noon	Pushed forward to CHELTENHAM ROAD keeping touch with Regt. on left. Received instructions to occupy positions near Cross Roads CHELTENHAM ROAD LYDDITE Lane.	
		12.15 pm	Instructions carried out and got in touch with C Coy on LA BASSEE Road.	
		4.45 pm	Received instructions to occupy positions on HAILEYBURY ROAD with C Coy in support on LA BASSEE Road.	
		5.20 pm	Coy and Platoon Commanders arranged to reconnoitre positions on HAILEYBURY Road but on arrival at Orchard in M.15.a.9.3 enemy commenced shelling the party very heavily. There were no casualties.	

Army Form C. 2118.

WAR DIARY
or
INTELLIGENCE SUMMARY.
(Erase heading not required.)

Instructions regarding War Diaries and Intelligence Summaries are contained in F. S. Regs., Part II. and the Staff Manual respectively. Title pages will be prepared in manuscript.

Place	Date	Hour	Summary of Events and Information	Remarks and references to Appendices
R.18.c.25.20	3/9/18	9 pm	D. Coy 7.45 p.m. Moved into position in front of HAILEYBURY ROAD. Got into touch with units on both flanks.	Innt
			Prisoners taken by the Battalion 1 officer (wounded) 1 other Ranks. Casualties. Other Ranks 1 B.S.W. 1 gassed. Weather excellent.	
M.14.c.50.00	4.9.18	9.1pm	At 11.55 a.m. orders were received from Brigade to advance to old British Front Line running from M.23.d.70.00 to N.7.d. origin. The Battalion advanced to this line in the following manner:—	
			A Coy 4 pm. Advanced in support to B. Coy to meet Objective.	
			6.0 pm In position as Regtl Support Coy from LONELY POST, RUE DU BACQUEROT including WINCHESTER POST and TILLELOY NORTH POST (Right of Sector) In touch with 2nd Bttn. WILTS Regt on Right.	
			B Coy 10.30 am. Advanced outpost line to a line running M.23.d.1.4 to M.15.d.7.1. Support relieved from 2 Platoons to 1 Platoon.	
			3.15 pm Advanced & established and consolidate line of posts on RUE TILLELOY from M.23.d.70 to M.24.b.3.9.	
			4.30 pm Arrived at M.29.b.7.9 where Coy came under observation from AUBERS RIDGE. Enemy shelled road fork and RUE TILLELOY also CHAPIGNY FARM.	
			5.0 pm Coy advanced N.E. from M.29.b.7.9 along RUE TILLELOY in following order. Advanced Guard No.7 Platoon. Nos. 5, C.H.Q. 6 and 8.	Innt

WAR DIARY
or
INTELLIGENCE SUMMARY.

Army Form C. 2118.

Place	Date	Hour	Summary of Events and Information	Remarks and references to Appendices
M.14.c.50.00	4/9/18	9 p.m.	B. Coy 5.15 p.m. No. 7 Platoon advanced to SNIPERS POST M.24.a.7.2. where they were engaged by M.Gs. from M.24.b.3.3. Estimated about 40 or 50 enemy at about M.24.b.3.3. Nos 7 and 5 Platoons withdrew covered by C.H.Q. who had disposed themselves for all round defence at CHAPIGNY FARM. Whilst this was in progress the Coy Commander reconnoitred our old front line at about M.24.c.5.2. and decided to consolidate here.	
		5.30 p.m.	Coy disposed as follows:- C.H.Q. and 6 Platoon at CHAPIGNY FARM Nos 5, 7, + 8 Platoons under cover in JOCK STREET, M.29.b.	
		5.45 p.m.	Located D. Coy H.Q. at M.18.d. 05.65.	
		6.0 p.m.	Reported situation to D. + A Coys and to Bttn. H.Q. Conferred with Platoon Commanders and on receiving the intelligence that 2nd Btn were R&R were not advancing across RUE TILLELOY decided to occupy the support line viz 3 Platoons keeping one in reserve in rear of DREADNOUGHT POST. At this time RUE TILLELOY from JOCK STREET to CHAPIGNY FARM was being heavily shelled by field + heavy guns. Party on account of 50% of these having N.C.O's. the Coy had only one N.C.O. slightly wounded.	
		7.30 p.m.	Under cover of fairly light proceeded to occupy support line running from M.23.d.3.3 and M.18.a.8.4. Platoons disposed in following order from Right to Left. Nos 8, 5, and 7. C.H.Q. and No 6 Platoon in rear of DREADNOUGHT POST.	

cont.

WAR DIARY or INTELLIGENCE SUMMARY

Army Form C. 2118.

Place	Date	Hour	Summary of Events and Information	Remarks and references to Appendices
M.14.c.50.00	4/9/18	9p.m.	C. Coy. 2.30 p.m. moved forward in support to D Coy and took up position on RUE DE BACQUEROT at R.17.b. holding MASSELOT and WANGERIE POSTS.	
		8.0 a.m.	D. Coy. Found the West Ridings (Btn on our left) had withdrawn about 800 yards.	
		12.45 p.m.	Received instructions to push forward and occupy posts on RUE TILLELOY. On receipt of these instructions the Coy. Cdr. got into touch with the WEST RIDINGS relaying them that he was advancing. The West Ridings had also received instructions to advance.	
		3 p.m.	The Coy in Artillery formation, covered by a reconnoitring screen advanced to position on RUE TILLELOY. No sign of the enemy was found until after crossing RUE DE BACQUEROT when he opened fire with 2 M.G.s. and a number of rifles. Coy halted. Upon Coy Cdr & Scouts had spent some time in reconnoitring the country the Platoons filtered into their positions up to the Communication Trench. Enemy commenced shelling but only one man was hit, presumably was experienced in getting into position owing to the activity of Enemy snipers, but by keeping as low as possible casualties were avoided. Enemy was found to be about 300 yards East of RUE TILLELOY. On posts our pickets were machiney (?) established (?) and send	
		7.40 p.m.	Instructions received to consolidate new position and send guides to incoming Battalion.	
		At 5.30 p.m.	Btn. received orders from 178th Bde for the relief of the Btn. by the 11th Bdn. ROYAL SCOTS FUSILIERS.	

WAR DIARY or INTELLIGENCE SUMMARY

Army Form C. 2118.

Place	Date	Hour	Summary of Events and Information	Remarks and references to Appendices
M.14.c.50.00	4/9/18	9 p.m.	Casualties. Officers 2nd Lieut J.A. SCOTT gassed slightly. Other Ranks. 1 gassed. 1 S.W. Weather excellent.	KWD
M.14.c.50.00	5/9/18 8 p.m.		The relief of this Bn by 11th Bn Royal Scots Fusiliers was reported complete at 8 a.m. Bn. in support to 11th. R.S.F. and is disposed as follows:— Left Support Coy. on Road M.14.a. Right Support Coy on Road M.21.c. Left Outpost Coy. 2 Platoons, M.14.a.9.2. 1 Plat. M.14.b.6.5. 1 Plat. M.14.a.3.5. Right " 2 " M.21.b.9.0. 1 " M.22.a.0.6. 1 " M.22.c.5.6. Casualties: Other Ranks Killed 2 (Suicide) G.S.W. 3. Gassed 1. Weather excellent.	KWD
do.	6.9.18	9 p.m.	Battalion in support – Resting. Casualties Nil. Weather good.	KWD
do.	7.9.18	do	Orders received from 178th Bde. to relieve 25th Kings Liverpool Regt. in Left Sub-Sector on the night 7/8th. September. Detachment of XI Corps Cyclists to be handed over to relieving Bn. Company of 13th. Duke of Wellingtons Regt. will be at the disposal of O.C. Commanding Officer, Company Commanders and Intelligence Officer visited Kings L'pool Regt to arrange details of relief. Casualties – Nil. Weather showery & cold. Very dark night.	KWD

WAR DIARY or INTELLIGENCE SUMMARY

Army Form C. 2118.

Place	Date	Hour	Summary of Events and Information	Remarks and references to Appendices
M.11.6. 95.87	8/9/18	9 p.m.	Relief of 25th. Bn. Kings L'pool Regt. completed at 2 a.m. Patrols report enemy occupying a newly dug trench about N.7.b.80.75. Enemy M.G. firing at N.8.a.1.4. An enemy working party heard at about N.I.a.8.2. and was dispersed by Lewis Gun fire. HYDE PARK clear of enemy and trench from HYDE PARK to PICCADILLY occupied. Country south of HYDE PARK open and affords no cover from view to the enemy. Casualties Nil. Weather showery & cold with high wind.	nil
do.	9/9/18	9 p.m.	Orders from 178th Bde received for the relief of the Bn. by 26th. Bn. Royal Welsh Fusiliers. On completion of relief the 178th. Bde. will be withdrawn to the Right Sector of the Corps Main Battle line. Patrols report enemy in Rural position. At 3.45 p.m. enemy commenced firing L.T.M. shells near WINDY POST from the direction of TWO TREE FARM. The Artillery was called upon to deal with this battery. On return of patrol it reported that when our guns commenced aire Germans ran out of a M.G. emplacement at N.1 d. 8.7. but before reaching cover 17 of them were hit. T.M. Battery was effectively silenced. Enemy fired about 50 shells - 77 m.m. calibre between 6.20 and 6.45 p.m. into D Coys position. The battery was observed at N.2.d.0.4 in a wood while the smoke was seen. Artillery called upon to retaliate, which it did effectively. Casualties - 2 other Ranks wounded. 2 O.R. missing. Weather bad. Wet, cold & stormy.	nil

Army Form C. 2118.

WAR DIARY
or
INTELLIGENCE SUMMARY.
(Erase heading not required.)

Instructions regarding War Diaries and Intelligence Summaries are contained in F. S. Regs., Part II. and the Staff Manual respectively. Title pages will be prepared in manuscript.

Place	Date	Hour	Summary of Events and Information	Remarks and references to Appendices
M 14 a 30.30	10.9.18	9 pm	Relief of this Btn. by 24th. Bn. Royal Irish Fusiliers completed at 6 am. The inclemency of the weather — very showery & pitch dark — made the relief very difficult. Battalion billeted in demolished houses & buildings on CHELTENHAM ROAD and ESTAIRES-LA BASSÉE ROAD. Very bad accommodation which is being improved as fast as possible by utilising old enemy Ammunition dumps shelters to patch up the buildings & damaged huts & dugouts. Casualties 1 Other Rk. missing. Weather bad.	Appx
do.	11.9.18	"	Battalion Resting. Improvements to billets being carried out. CHARTERHOUSE POST shelled during the night, where C. Company is billeted. Casualties other Ranks 1 killed 3 wounded. Weather still very bad.	Appx
do.	12.9.18	"	Battalion resting. Casualties Nil. Weather bad – showery & wet.	
do.	13.9.18	"	" " Many sick are reporting. The sick reports for the past three days are as follows:— 11th, 31. 12th, 58. 13th, 99. Casualties Nil. Weather a little improved — still showery & very cold.	Appx
do.	14.9.18	"	Battalion resting. The roads are in a very bad condition owing to the heavy rainfall during the past few days. Fatigue parties detailed for scraping the surface. Casualties Nil. Sick on the increase, 121 reported today. Weather very wet and cold.	Appx

WAR DIARY
or
INTELLIGENCE SUMMARY.

Army Form C. 2118.

(Erase heading not required).

Place	Date	Hour	Summary of Events and Information	Remarks and references to Appendices
M.4.a.20.30	15.9.18	9pm	Battalion still resting, Church service held this morning. Casualties Nil. Weather completely changed, very bright and warm.	kept
do.	16.9.18	9pm	Battalion digging defences, wiring, and training. The Battalion area was shelled during the night 15/16th with Shrapnel, Gas, and H.E. Casualties Other Ranks 3 G.S.W. Weather excellent	kept
do.	17.9.18	9pm	Battalion engaged in digging defences and training. Casualties Other Ranks 1 G.S.W. Weather excellent	kept
do.	18.9.18	9pm	Battalion engaged in making defences & training. Casualties Nil. Weather excellent.	kept
do.	19.9.18	9pm	As for yesterday. Casualties Nil. Weather Good.	kept
do.	20.9.18	9pm	Battalion training and engaged on the construction of defences. Casualties Other Ranks 1 G.S.W. 1 Gassed	kept
do.	21.9.18	9pm	178th Infy Bde Order No 134 received. "The 176th Inf. Bde will relieve the 177th Inf. Bde. as previously Scout Regiment from night 22/23rd September" 1/36th Works Frans. will relieve the 15th Essex Regt on the left Sub Sector. Commanding Officer, Adjutant, & Coy. Commanders and Intelligence Officer visited 11th Essex Regt to arrange details of relief & to keep look over the Sector. Battalion still constructing defences, wiring &c. Casualties Nil. Weather Fair	kept

WAR DIARY
or
INTELLIGENCE SUMMARY.
(Erase heading not required.)

Army Form C. 2118.

Place	Date	Hour	Summary of Events and Information	Remarks and references to Appendices
M12a.50.90 Sheet 36 SW1	22/9/18	9pm	Battalion Headquarters moved from M.14.a.30.30 to HARLECH CASTLE M.12.a.50.90. The relief of 11th. Battalion Essex Regt. in the Left Sector was completed and in progress from 8pm. Casualties Nil. Weather very good.	King
do.	23/9/18	9pm	The relief of 11th Bn. Essex Regt was completed at 12.30 a.m. Battalion holding front from M.7.d. origin to N.1.b.70.80. On our Right is the 11th. Bn. Royal Scots Fusiliers, on our Left, a Bn. of East Lancs. Regt. Casualties Other Ranks G.S.W. 3. Weather fair	King
do.	24/9/18	9pm	Battalion in the line. Casualties O.R. 3 G.S.W. Weather fair	King
do.	25/9/18	9pm	178th. Infty. Bde. Order No. 136 received. This order informs us that 100 drums C.G. will be fired from projectors to inflict casualties and cause a disturbance. Firing position M.6.d.5.4. Targets N.1.d.2.5. M.11.39 p.m. 296th. Brigade R.F.A. fired a crash on TWO TREE FARM and continued firing at a slower rate for 5 minutes. At 11.40 pm the projectors were fired simultaneously. ("M" Special Coy. R.E.) At 11.45 p.m. the Officer in charge of the operation reported that the operation was complete and guns aeroplane. Patrols report M.6.d at N.7.d. 6.5. No enemy encountered. Casualties Nil. Weather fair.	King

WAR DIARY
or
INTELLIGENCE SUMMARY.

(Erase heading not required.)

Army Form C. 2118.

Place	Date	Hour	Summary of Events and Information	Remarks and references to Appendices
M.12.a.50.90 Sheet 36 S.W.1.	24/9/18	9 p.m.	Uneventful day. At 10 p.m. Artillery fired a crash on Right Btn. front of Bn. Bruin. In retaliation the enemy bombarded the Btn. area. At Casualties 1 O.R. G.S.W. Weather fair.	Nil
do.	27/9/18	9 p.m.	At 3 a.m. and lasting till 3.40 a.m. an enemy bombarded Battalion area with Gas & H.E. shells. Enemy artillery has been active throughout the day. Casualties Nil. Weather good.	Nil
do.	28/9/18	9 p.m.	At 1.30 p.m. message received from 178th Brigade that the Btn. would be relieved by 2 Battns. of 176th Brigade, 17th Bn. R. Sussex Regt. on the Right and 25th Bn. Kings L'pool Regt. on Left. At 4.50 p.m. message cancelling the previous one arrived and informed us that the 26th Battalion Royal Welch Fusiliers would relieve this Battalion, and that we should take over the blocks evacuated by 26th R.W.F on completion of relief. The Battalion area was shelled during the day and (A Coy. Right Front Coy.) suffered casualties. Other Ranks 2 killed 5 G.S.W. Weather very cold and showery.	Nil
		8.10 p.m.	A message was received from Brigade as follows :- "No operations scheduled to recapture 7000 prisoners taken. You will hold our patrols to return not later than 2 a.m. to get in touch with enemy and forces must be carried with enemy and we are not content to be left behind."	

Army Form C. 2118.

WAR DIARY
or
INTELLIGENCE SUMMARY.
(Erase heading not required.)

Instructions regarding War Diaries and Intelligence Summaries are contained in F. S. Regs., Part II. and the Staff Manual respectively. Title pages will be prepared in manuscript.

Place	Date	Hour	Summary of Events and Information	Remarks and references to Appendices
Sheet 36a S.E.2. R.3.d.40.10.	29.9.18	9 p.m.	At 10.45 p.m. Two patrols left to get in touch with enemy. The relief of this Btn. by 26th. Batt. Royal Welch Fusiliers was completed by 1.10 a.m. The two patrols returned at 2 p.m. and 2.20 p.m. respectively. The patrol that went out from the Right Front Company reported an enemy M.G. firing from the orchard near JOCKS LODGE. The patrol from Left Front Company reported an enemy working party digging about N.1.a.50.50 and that they were coughing and other noises to indicate the presence of the enemy very plainly were fired at close range and even the party were fired on by a M.G. The officers in command of the patrols held that M.Gs. were firing from their usual positions and is certain that the enemy has not moved any withdrawal from his forward positions. Battalion in billets at PONT RIQUEL resting. Weather very cold. Casualties Nil.	Kingd
do.	30.9.18	9 p.m.	Battalion in billets - resting. Casualties Nil. Weather very wet & cold.	Kingd

J.F. Thompson. Lt. Col.
Commanding 26th. Btn. North'd Fusrs.

ORIGINAL

Vol 7

36TH N.F.'S.
WAR DIARY
OCT 1918.

SECRET

To:- "Q" Qr.
   178th Inf. Bde.

36TH BATTN.
NORTHUMBERLAND
FUSILIERS.
No. 360/12/B
Date 31.10.18

Herewith Original
copy of War Diary
for October 1918

J.T. Thompson Lt. Col.
       C.O. q 36 N.F.

Army Form C. 2118.

WAR DIARY
or
INTELLIGENCE SUMMARY. 36 Northumberland Fusiliers.
(Erase heading not required.)

Place	Date	Hour	Summary of Events and Information	Remarks and references to Appendices
PONT RIQUEL R.3.a.40.10 Sheet 36a S.E.2.	1.10.18	9pm	Battalion resting. Improving billets, bathing, &c. Casualties Nil. Weather improved.	Kind
do.	2.10.18	9pm	178th. Infy. Bde. Order No 141 received - as follows. "178th. Infy. Bde. will relieve 182nd Infty. Bde. in the left section of W.d. Divne. front tomorrow night between 2/3rd. 28th. R. Welch Fusrs. and one Coy 36th. North'd Fusrs will relieve 2/8th. Worcs. Rgt. and 2/6th. Warwickshire Rgt. in the front line. 36th. North'd Fusrs. less one Coy. will relieve 2/7th. Warwickshire Rgt. in Brigade Support. On completion of relief 26th. R. Welch Fusrs. who have 3 Coys in front line one Coy. in right support and the Coy of 36th. North'd Fusrs. in left support will relieve the Coy of 36th. North'd Fusrs. now in G.8.a. (BOIS GRENIER Sheet)". "B" Coy of this Battalion is attached to 28th. R. Welch Fusrs. Entrained at LESTREM church at 6/pm. Headquarters, D.A. and C Coys marched to the new area G.8.a. arriving there at 7.30 /pm. The relief of 2/7th. Warwickshire was complete at 8.45/pm. Casualties Nil. Weather Good.	Kind

Army Form C. 2118.

WAR DIARY
or
INTELLIGENCE SUMMARY. 36th Northumberland Fusiliers
(Erase heading not required.)

Instructions regarding War Diaries and Intelligence Summaries are contained in F. S. Regs., Part II. and the Staff Manual respectively. Title pages will be prepared in manuscript.

Place	Date	Hour	Summary of Events and Information	Remarks and references to Appendices
G.18.a.2.1. Sht 36 N.W.	3.10.18	9 p.m.	Instructions received from 178th Infty Bde. to move at 8 a.m. to the area YORK POST - RUE BATAILLE POST, TWENTIETH POST FORT ROMPU, with Bn. H.Q. at G.18.a.2.1. The move was completed at 10.45 a.m.	
H.18.a.20.10			At 11.30 a.m. instructions from 178th Bde received ordering the Battalion to move not later than 3 p.m. as follows. 1 Company FLEURIE SWITCH J.13. 2 Companies FLEURBAIX-HOUPLINES line H.23.17.18 and 12.a.d. Bn H.Q. H.18.a.20.10. A. Coy. L'ARMÉE POST H.18.b.1. C. Coy in FLEURIE SWITCH, D. Coy in trenches H.18.a and one platoon in RED HOUSE POST H.24.b.1. Casualties Nil. Weather very cold & damp.	Kml
H.36.a.60.50 to	4.10.18	9 p.m.	Verbal instructions from Brigade received to the effect that the Bn. would be relieved by the Royal Sussex Regt. before nightfall. At 1.30 p.m. instructions for Guides to conduct Royal Sussex Regt. known Coy & H.Q. despatches to report to R.S. H.Q. at 15.30. The relief of the Bn by the Royal Sussex Regt. was completed at 6 p.m. & 3 Coys & Bn. H.Q. marched to hutts on road running from ROUGE DE BOUT to RUE de BLANCHE. "B" Coy was relieved from 28th R. Welsh Fus. & spent the night at H.18.a.20.10 marching into the Bn. area the following day. Casualties Nil. Weather dull & very cold.)	Kml

Army Form C. 2118.

WAR DIARY
or
INTELLIGENCE SUMMARY. 26th Northumberland Fusiliers
(Erase heading not required.)

Instructions regarding War Diaries and Intelligence Summaries are contained in F.S. Regs., Part II. and the Staff Manual respectively. Title pages will be prepared in manuscript.

Place	Date	Hour	Summary of Events and Information	Remarks and references to Appendices
H.26.a.60.50. Sheet 36.N.W.	5/10/18	9pm	Battalion in billets - denoused enemy shelters & dugouts etc. Resting, & improving billets - bathing. Casualties Nil. Weather dull & cold.	hsp.
do.	6/10/18	9pm	Battalion resting. Casualties Nil. - Weather bad.	hsp.
do.	7/10/18	9pm	Battalion resting - improving billets etc. Weather very cold & damp. Casualties Nil.	hsp.
do.	8/10/18	9pm	Major Genl. N.M. SMYTH, V.C., C.B., Commanding 59th. Divn. inspected the Btn. and presented decorations to Capt. R.S. HADDON, (Comdg. No 4 Platoon) FLEMING (Comdg No 4 Platoon) Military Crosses. Corporal A.T. KEYWORTH A. Coy and Pte E. PANKHURST with the Military Medal. These decorations were earned on Sept. 3rd in the advance on LAVENTIE. Casualties Nil.	hsp.
do.	9/10/18	9pm	Battalion training Casualties Nil. Weather fair	hsp.
do.	10/10/18	9pm	No 178 Inf. Bde Order No 1412 received. "178th. Infy Bde. relieves 177th. Inf. Bde. in left sector of Brunefront, on night 10/11th. October. 36th. North'd Fus. relieve 15th. Rtn. Essex Rgt. in Right Sub-sector. 36th. N.F. route for relief any route South of Erie line between H.22 and 28." The Battalion moved off at 1730 hours Casualties Nil. Weather good	hsp.

Army Form C. 2118.

WAR DIARY
or
INTELLIGENCE SUMMARY. 36th Northumberland Fusiliers

(Erase heading not required.)

Place	Date	Hour	Summary of Events and Information	Remarks and references to Appendices
I.32.c.40.00. Sheet 36 N.W	11.10.18	9 p.m.	The Battalion relieved 15th. Sussex Regt. at 9.30 p.m. 10.10.18. Dispositions of the Bn. as follows. Rear Bn. H.Q. at H.36.c.60.20. Advanced Coy H.Q. at I.32.c.40.00. Rear B.H.Q. 2nd in Command, Readjust Hdq. M.O. and Chaplain. Ad. Advanced B.H.Q. Commanding Officer, Adjutant, Intelligence Officer and Artillery Liaison Officer. H. Coy. One platoon in front in line of posts as follows, Liaison post I.34.c.30.00. Rifle Post I.34.c.40.25. Double Lewis Gun Post at I.34.c.70.50. Rifle Post I.34.a.70.05. One Platoon behind Railway Embankment I.34.c. Two platoons in reserve in INCUBATOR TRENCH I.33.b. and d. D. Coy. One platoon in front line in line of posts Rifle & Lewis Gun alternately in INCLINE STREET I.34.a. Liaison Post at I.28.c.70.45. One platoon in reserve in "INCOME DRIVE" I.33.a. Joint Coy. H.Q. of A. & D Coys. in concrete "Pillbox" at I.33.b.55.75. I.31.b. B. and C. Coys in reserve in areas I.32.a. and I.31.b. On our Right the 20th London Regt. (47th. Divn.) On our left 13th. Duke of Wellingtons Regt. Instructions from Brigade that patrols are to keep in touch with enemy as this is a possibility of his retiring. At dawn this morning patrols went out and found him holding the ridge with M.Gs and Snipers posts. Casualties 2 R.S.W. One stretcher caused by dugout being blown in. All other ranks. Weather Good.	

Army Form C. 2118.

WAR DIARY
or
INTELLIGENCE SUMMARY. 26th Northumberland Fusiliers
(Erase heading not required.)

Instructions regarding War Diaries and Intelligence Summaries are contained in F.S. Regs., Part II and the Staff Manual respectively. Title pages will be prepared in manuscript.

Place	Date	Hour	Summary of Events and Information	Remarks and references to Appendices.
T.32.c.40.00.	12.10.18	9 p.m.	Quiet day. Dawn patrols report enemy in same positions. Casualties Nil. Weather very wet + cold.	kept
do.	13.10.18	9 p.m.	Dawn patrol returned with one prisoner taken from a M.G. post at I.29.b.20.50. Brigade inform us that much useful information has been obtained from him. Brigdr. Genl. STANSFIELD L D Coming 178 Bde. sent a congratulatory wire to Lieut. A.T. BRADLEY who was in command of the patrol. A message received from Rose. States that from information received from prisoners a retirement on a very large scale is to take place tonight. This Btn. and Btn. on left instructed to send out nominate patrols to be back by 2 a.m. At 5 a.m. a strong patrol of one platoon covered by a screen and supported by a second platoon to be sent out by this Btn. and Btn. on left, and to make every effort to obtain a prisoner. All units warned to prepare to advance tomorrow. Casualties Nil. Weather good.	kept
do.	14.10.18	9 p.m.	At 11 p.m. last night issued the following order. "Morning order. No ordinary patrols to be out after 0200 hours. All Coys. will stand to ready to advance at 0400 hours. The word MOVE. A + D Coys. will advance to first objective in following formation. Platoon each covered by screen in front line at more interval, followed by 100 yds. distance. Platoons by a second platoon each in more formation 200 yds distance. Platoons	

Army Form C. 2118.

WAR DIARY
or
INTELLIGENCE SUMMARY. 30th Northumberland Fusiliers

(Erase heading not required.)

Instructions regarding War Diaries and Intelligence Summaries are contained in F. S. Regs., Part II. and the Staff Manual respectively. Title pages will be prepared in manuscript.

Place	Date	Hour	Summary of Events and Information	Remarks and references to Appendices
I.32.c.40.00	10/10/18	9 p.m.	at present in support will advance in line bespread. Battalion frontage as already given out. Keep connection with units on flanks and between Coys. Road brushed, houses, &. enemy examined. Screen the supplies with same owing Bomb C. Coys on receipt of MOVE will at once occupy dispositions of present forward Companies and await orders. B.H.Q. will remain as at present. Relaxation will be communicated tout Coys. A & D Coys to report by quickest method occupation of first objective also progress each half hour. Relay posts two cycles in position in I 33.6.4.5 to follow advance of A + D Coys via cross roads in I 34.c. over I 34 6. 70. 95" via road S.E. direction I 35" central. Acknowledge."

At 5 a.m. the patrols went forward. A Coy on right was held up on the ridge with M.G and rifle fire. However the Battalion on the Right did not advance thus necessitating the formation of a defensive flank on the right from the ridge to the London Regts. left post. D Coys patrol advanced over the ridge into the sunken road running through I 35 a.6.0. without meeting any opposition. The enemy were completely demoralized and held up their hands. 4 M.G. and 6 prisoners were first of all captured & sent back. A further party of 15 were advanced back from lines but eventually arrived at the West Riding hands. There on our arrival at sunken road mentioned above that the parties of the West [struck through] Redoups (The Ren on our left) having moved up with [illegible] our men and from then onwards many of the West Ridings Regt. men | |

WAR DIARY
or
INTELLIGENCE SUMMARY.
(Erase heading not required.)

Army Form C. 2118.

5th Northumberland Fusiliers

Hour, Date, Place	Summary of Events and Information	Remarks and references to Appendices
I.32.c.40.00. 14.10.18. 9 p.m.	The command of my two officers. At I.35.c.4.6. a party of enemy including 3 officers were seen emerging from a concrete pillbox. They immediately surrendered with the exception of one man who refused to come out. A Mills bomb was thrown in the pillbox. During this time many of the enemy were killed and their demoralis-ation was complete. After clearing this dugout the party went about 100 yards east of the sunken road. It was here that the enemy counter attacked. An officer leading a party was seen coming along a hedge at I.35.c.2.5. They took up a position on the was after and a M.G. Bun men had to retire before fire from the sunken road. It was then that the enemy succeeded in outflanking our party which then always to withdraw on reaching I.35.a.1.1. just east of enemy trench it was found impossible to reach our line owing to enfilade M.G. fire from the flanks. It was then about 6.30 a.m. The enemy were heard to cheer and commenced coming over the ridge in line for a charge. Up his own men had sustained only 10 casualties and had shot in possession of Lewis Guns which when turned on the enemy caused them to retire. The enemy made several attempts to close around the party but each time was repulsed, and they must have sustained very severe losses. Our casualties were increasing, most officers being carried by enemy snipers who climbed trees & shot down our men.	

Army Form C. 2118.

WAR DIARY
or
INTELLIGENCE SUMMARY. 36th Northumberland Fusiliers
(Erase heading not required.)

Instructions regarding War Diaries and Intelligence Summaries are contained in F.S. Regs., Part II. and the Staff Manual respectively. Title pages will be prepared in manuscript.

Hour, Date, Place	Summary of Events and Information	Remarks and references to Appendices
I 32. c. 40. 00. 14.10.18 9 p.m.	Our wounded who attempted to regain our lines were invariably shot down. This portion of acre continued all morning. About 7 a.m. enemy put down a heavy box barrage around the party and again the enemy was heard cheering. At 12.15 p.m. our artillery opened fire and under cover of this barrage and our M.G. fire the two officers decided to make a dash for our lines. During this run several men were hit and several evacuated sustained fresh wounds. The survivors who reached our line untouched were 17 out of a total of 42 who started. Total casualties killed 5, wounded 9 missing 11. Captures 21 prisoners and one machine gun. We also had 4 Lewis guns. Orders for the relief of this Battn. by 11th. R. Scots Fusrs. received. Relief was completed at 8.30 p.m. Casualties 27. Other Ranks. Weather very good	Kind.
H 27. d. 10. 85. 15.10.18. 9 p.m.	Battalion resting. Casualties Nil. Weather dull and cold	Kind
I 33. 6. 50. 75. 16.10.18. 9 p.m.	Telephone message from Brigade, that 11th. Scots Fusrs & 15th. West Ridings had gone forward and this Battalion was to move forward in close support. At 9.30 a.m. Battn.	

Army Form C. 2118.

WAR DIARY
or
INTELLIGENCE SUMMARY. 38th Northumberland Fusiliers
(Erase heading not required.)

Place	Hour, Date	Summary of Events and Information	Remarks and references to Appendices
I.33.b.55.70.	16.10.18. 9pm.	Moved forward and took up position vacated by 11th R. Scots Fus. Bttn. H.Q. I.33.b.55.70. A. Coy. I.32.b. B. Coy. I.33.b. and d. C. Coy. I.21. I.27.a. and I.27.b. D. Coy. I.27.a. Bttn in position at 1.30 p.m. Casualties Nil. Weather very wet.	Init.
LOMME J.27.c.40.25. Sheet 36 N.E.3.	17.10.18. 9pm.	At 11.20 last night instructions from Brigade received warning this Bttn to be prepared to move at one hours notice after 9.30 a.m. 17th instant. At 2.30 p.m. in accordance with instructions received from Bde during the morning the Bttn. moved forward to LOMME and halted there for the night. During the forenoon 9 bodies were reported on the site of the operations on 15th inst. and were buried at I.33.6.55.70. One man Pte. STEPHENSON was still alive when picked up and was re-dressed and sent to Hospital.	Init.
FLIERS. TOURNAI Sheet 5. A.5.A.6.6	18.10.18. 9pm.	During previous night orders received to move to R.28.6.7.7 Sheet 36. N.E. The Battalion moved off at 8.30 a.m. reaching K.20.d. at 10.30 a.m. Bttn going to the bridges over the HAUTE DEULE canal being destroyed the Bttn was held up here until 3 p.m. At this time one bridge was completed sufficiently to allow passage for infantry, as the Bttn was to be transport

Army Form C. 2118.

WAR DIARY
or
INTELLIGENCE SUMMARY. 36th Northumberland Fusiliers

(Erase heading not required.)

Instructions regarding War Diaries and Intelligence Summaries are contained in F.S. Regs., Part II. and the Staff Manual respectively. Title pages will be prepared in manuscript.

Hour, Date, Place	Summary of Events and Information	Remarks and references to Appendices
FLERS, TOURNAI Sheet 5. 5. A. 5. b. 9 p.m.	moved to cross roads LA MADELEINE K.28 b.7.7. At 4.30 p.m. verbal instructions were received from Staff Capt. 178th Bde. to push on to FLERS where Brigade H.Q. was established. The Bttn reached FLERS at about 6.30 p.m. and men were billeted in the village. The transport arrived at 9 p.m.	init.
TEMPLEUVE. H.33.a.7.4. Sheet 37	19.10.18. 9 p.m. At 10.30 a.m. Orders were received from 178th Bde. for this Bttn. to be on line of road running N.E. and S.W. R.3.G. and C by 07.30 hours and move forward from there astride the gap between 11th R.S.F. and 13th. West Ridings is fixed by 09.30. At 4.30 a.m. the following orders were received:— "178th. Inf. Bde. will continue the advance today in conjunction with Bdes. on Right & left. Objectives allotted to 59th. Divn. WILLEMS – SAILLY LES LENNOY line TREU DEWAZON - TEMPLEUVE HOLONS ZH.21.C. The Bttn. will advance at 07.00 and will make a further advance from first objective at 13.00. 36th. N.F. will be in position W of BOIS D'ANAPPES at 06.00 and were free gap between 11th R.S.F. and Bde. on left by 07.45." Bttn was in position N east of BOIS D'ANAPPES at advanced from there at 07.45 and gained the first objective by 12 noon meeting with no opposition. The advance from WILLEMS was continued at 13.35	

0000 should read
1000. See War appendix
14 in 11/R.S.F diary (178?
Bde) for oct: 1918

WAR DIARY
INTELLIGENCE SUMMARY. 36th Northumberland Fusiliers

Army Form C. 2118.

(Erase heading not required.)

Hour, Date, Place	Summary of Events and Information	Remarks and references to Appendices
TEMPLEUVE, H.33.a.7.4. Sheet 37, 19.10.18 9pm	and final objective was reached at 4.30pm. The line being held just the foreign line of posts from H.34.a.5.0 along road running N.W. through H.34.a. H.33.b. H.27.a. to H.27.b. Central. B. and C. Coys in front line and A & D Coys in close support. In touch with Royal Fusiliers Regt. on left at H.26.b.1.0. and with 11th R.S.F. on the right. Casualties Nil. weather cold & wet.	Nil.
H.30.d.00.40 Sheet 37 20-10-18 9pm.	At 0415 instructions from 178th Bde arrived as follows:- "Bde will advance to line of TOURNAI-TURCOING Railway 1000 yards and eastward push forward to river L'ESCAUT with posts on the eastern bank." Detailed instructions follow. later the following instructions were received:- "The Brigade will effect a crossing at PONT A CHIN and establish a bridgehead. 36th N.F. + 11th R.S.F. will advance at 0000 to the general line N.5.b. H.29.d. 11th R.S.F. will be prepared to form a defensive flank facing BLANDAIN. From this line each Btn. will send forward a strong patrol supported by infantry and machine guns to ascertain the enemy dispositions in the woods lining the Western bank of the ESCAUT. Later 36th N.F. will effect a crossing at PONT A CHIN and 11th R.S.F. will ascertain if there are any bridges on his front. Pontoons cannot be used until the situation is cleaner."	

WAR DIARY
or
INTELLIGENCE SUMMARY 1st Northumberland Fusiliers

Army Form C. 2118.

(Erase heading not required.)

Hour, Date, Place	Summary of Events and Information	Remarks and references to Appendices
H.30.d.00.40 Sheet 37	20.10.18 9 p.m. At 10.30 hours the following orders were issued:— Companies will move in the direction and formation already detailed. On reaching N.5.b and H.29.a. general line will be established throughout the Brigade. Formation of leading companies to be none diamond; support companies two lines consisting of 2 platoons each at 100 yards distance. N. & S. company boundaries as given to be maintained as necessary. Special care being taken to guard flanks. On adjusting from line as given in para. 2, each forward company will send forward strong recce. patrols well supported to ascertain enemy dispositions on W. & E. bank L'ESCAUT, also possibilities for crossing L'ESCAUT. B.H.Q. will follow support Coys. in route given previously." The Bttn. moved in accordance with above orders and met with practically no resistance until after the railway had been crossed. On reaching the road PECQ – PONT A CHIN strong resistance was encountered from enemy M.G. fire. At 5 p.m. enemy put down a heavy barrage in region of PONT ACHIN and RAMEGNIES-CHIN. Bttn. H.Q. which had been established at L.31.b.1.9. had to move on account of heavy shelling to H.30.d.00.40	

WAR DIARY
or
INTELLIGENCE SUMMARY. 36th Northumberland Fusiliers

Army Form C. 2118.

(Erase heading not required.)

Hour, Date, Place	Summary of Events and Information	Remarks and references to Appendices
H.30.d.00.40. Sheet 37. 20.10.18 9p.m.	It was found that the bridge at PONT. a CHIN was destroyed and impassable. Posts were established covering R.town from our Western bank of the river and Companies established in positions as follows. A. Coy. PONT A CHIN. D. Coy. RAMEGNIES- CHIN. C. & B Coys. in billets in RAMEGNIES. Casualties Other Ras. G.S.W. 2. Weather wet & cold	fwd fwd
do. 21.10.18 9p.m.	At 6.30 a.m. the following order received from 178th. Bde. "On 21st. Brigade in conjunction with 57th. Divn. and 176th. Inf. Bde. is to effect crossing of the ESCAUT and later gain the high ground in I.25. 36th. N.F. and 11th. R.S.F. will cross the river and gain line TOURNAI- HERINEES Rly by 10.00. Preliminary groups were put down a barrage at 0900 from line 400 yds West of Rly. to Rly. from 0930 to 0945 no fire west of railway. 0945 on road through 04 a I 34.c. and I 27A. Crossing will be effected at PONT A CHIN and I 26 c. Necessary reconnaissance of these points were be carried out. At 1200 36th. N.F. were ordered to line of roads I 34 a and I 27 d. 11th. R.S.F. were to form a strong defensive flank on I 34 a 4.0. back forms in O 2 b. From this line 36th. N.F. were more forward and established posts about I 30 central. I 34.6.0.7. I 28.a.0.3.	fwd

WAR DIARY
or
INTELLIGENCE SUMMARY.

Army Form C. 2118.

36th Northumberland Fusiliers

(Erase heading not required.)

Hour, Date, Place	Summary of Events and Information	Remarks and references to Appendices
H.30.d. 00.40. Sheet 57. H.30.d. 00.40. 9 p.m.	The bridge at PONT A CHIN being destroyed it was impossible to get men over in daylight. 3 men made the crossing but it was very slow as this was in a depth of 10 feet in the middle. Reconnaissance of I.26.a shewed no possible place to effect a crossing. At 9.30 the enemy shelled the whole area very heavily and continued todo so throughout the day. The enemy was not affected by the afternoon rain reports to Brigade. L'ESCAUT River could not be crossed on pontoons as there was very swift water + very steep mud - in some places 15 feet deep. About 12 noon a telephone message from Bde informed us that the Btn was being relieved by a unit of 75th Divn. The relief commenced at 6.45 p.m. and at 7.15 p.m. the following wire was received. JUGU was to be relieved tonight by a Brigade of 75th Divn. On completion of relief PAFA (30.N.7) will be disposed H.25.c and d. H.32.a. The relief was completed at 8.50 p.m. Weather bad. Casualties Other Ranks G.S.W. 2.	Nil.

WAR DIARY
or
INTELLIGENCE SUMMARY.

Army Form C. 2118.

35th Northumberland Fusiliers

(Erase heading not required.)

Instructions regarding War Diaries and Intelligence Summaries are contained in F.S. Regs., Part II. and the Staff Manual respectively. Title pages will be prepared in manuscript.

Place	Hour, Date.	Summary of Events and Information	Remarks and references to Appendices
NECHIN H14 c.70.60.	22nd.10.18 9 p.m.	Verbal instructions received from Staff Capt. 178 Bde that the Bn was to move to NECHIN area as the area previously allotted to the Bn was insufficient to accommodate all Coy. C Coy had to march into NECHIN last night on this account. By 6 p.m. the battalion was in huts in NECHIN area. Casualties Nil. Weather improved.	Nil.
do.	23.10.18 9 p.m.	Battalion resting. Casualties Nil. Weather fair.	Nil.
do.	24.10.18 9 p.m.	At midnight an order from Brigade received ordering the Bn to be ready to move on ½ an hours notice from 9am. without transport. At 1230 hours 178th Infy Bde. Order No 145 received:- "The capture of MONT DE LA TRINITÉ will be carried out by the 177th Infy Bde. supported by 178th Inf Bde. and 176th Inf Bde. was in Bde. Reserve. 177th Infy Bde. will advance by bounds. First Objective - TOURNAI - HERINNES Railway Second Objective - HAVRON - ORGIES road to I.9.d.1.1. thence along railway to Northern Boundary. - - - 36th. Works there in to be in Bde. Reserve in I.27, I.13. and I.19. Right Boundary I.27. central. I.24.d.O.O. Left Boundary I.7. central. I.12 central.	

Army Form C. 2118.

WAR DIARY
or
INTELLIGENCE SUMMARY. 38th Northumberland Fusiliers

(Erase heading not required.)

Instructions regarding War Diaries and Intelligence Summaries are contained in F.S. Regs., Part II and the Staff Manual respectively. Title pages will be prepared in manuscript.

Hour, Date, Place	Summary of Events and Information	Remarks and references to Appendices
NECHIN. H.14.c.7.6. Sheet 37. 24th 10.18 9 p.m.	The Bn will be ready to move at half an hours notice. Bns will carry on their normal routine. Bns may take their Lewis Gun Limbers and Cookers as far as the river. On receipt of the above order an Officer from each Coy was sent forward to reconnaissance areas F.13 and F.19 with a view to training the accommodation therein. The Officers returned & found that the Bns at present in that area had not moved nor was there any immediate prospect of their doing so. This being so the transport were parked nearby & move if required & orders were issued to Coys for the men to return to their billets & sleep in a normal manner. Casualties Nil. Weather good.	Lieut.
TOUFFLERS C.22.c.4.4 Sheet 37. 25.10.18 9 p.m.	Orders from 178th Bde received ordering the Bn to take over of NECHIN by evening. H.Q., D & C Coys moved to billets in TOUFFLERS arriving about 7 p.m. Casualties Nil. Weather good.	Lieut.
do. 26.10.18 9 p.m.	Battalion training. Casualties Nil. Weather good.	Lieut.

Army Form C. 2118.

WAR DIARY
or
INTELLIGENCE SUMMARY. 36th Northumberland Fusiliers

(Erase heading not required.)

Place	Date	Hour	Summary of Events and Information	Remarks and references to Appendices
TOUFFLERS. G.22.c.4.4. Sheet 37	27.10.18	9 pm	Battalion resting. Casualties Nil. Weather good	Nil
do.	28.10.18	9 pm	Battalion training. Casualties Nil. Weather good	Nil
do.	29.10.18	9 pm	Battalion training. Casualties Nil. Weather good	Nil
do.	30.10.18	9 pm	Battalion training. Casualties Nil. Weather good	Nil
do.	31.10.18	9 pm	Battalion training. Casualties Nil. Weather good	Nil

J.Y. Nelson Lt. Col.
Commanding 36th Northumberland Fusiliers

CONFIDENTIAL.

WAR DIARY

36d Batt: NORTHUMBERLAND FUSLRS.

November 1918.

November 1918.   36 Northumberland Fusiliers

WAR DIARY
or
INTELLIGENCE SUMMARY

Army Form C. 2118.

(Erase heading not required.)

Instructions regarding War Diaries and Intelligence Summaries are contained in F.S. Regs., Part II. and the Staff Manual respectively. Title pages will be prepared in manuscript.

Place	Date	Hour	Summary of Events and Information	Remarks and references to Appendices
TOUFFLERS G.22.b.4.4. Sheet 37	1-11-18	9 pm	Battalion training. Casualties Nil. Weather good	
do.	2/11/18	9 pm	do. Casualties Nil. Weather good	
do.	3-11-18	9 pm	Divine service. Casualties Nil. Weather good	
do.	4-11-18	9 pm	Battalion training. Casualties Nil. Weather good	
do.	5-11-18	9 pm	At 11 am wire received from 178th Bde instructing Bn to be prepared to move at shortest notice. Further wire received ordering billeting parties to be at church in NECHIN one hour after the word "MOVE" had been received. Battalion training. Casualties Nil. Weather good. Notification from Brigade received that the Bn was not likely to move today but to be in readiness to move at shortest notice from Brigade tomorrow.	
do.	6-11-18	9 pm	Battalion training. No word received to move. At 3 pm wire from Bde received "Situation remains unchanged PAFA (36 Nth N.F.) Serve relieve PAWO (1/1th Somerset L.I.) in Brigade reserve on 8/9. Reconnoitring parties should go forward tomorrow." Casualties Nil. Weather very bad, pouring rain.	

November 1918   26th Northumberland Army Form C. 2118.

WAR DIARY
or
INTELLIGENCE SUMMARY.
(Erase heading not required.)

Place	Date	Hour	Summary of Events and Information	Remarks and references to Appendices
TOUFFLERS G.22.c.4.4.	7.11.18	9pm	Reconnoitering parties proceed to HOLAINS to billets occupied by 11th. Somerset Light Infantry. Battalion training. Weather bad. Casualties Nil. 178th Infty. Bde. Order No 146 received.	Nil
HOLAINS H.20.d.50.80.	8.11.18	9pm	At 7am, 178th Infty. Bde. with relieve the 171st Infty Bde on the line our the night 8/9th November. 11th. Royal Scots Fusiliers will relieve 24th. D.L.I. on Right Subsection. 13th. Duke of Wellingtons will relieve 15th Sussex Regt. in Left Subsection. 36th. Northd Fus. will relieve 11th. S.L.I. in Batt. Reserve. Battalions will move off from their present billets as early as visibility and light allows. "——" Should the enemy retire tomorrow Battalions will carry out the tasks decided between us "Advance Instructions No. I. dated 6th November." The relief of 11th. Somerset Light Infty. was completed by 7pm. Casualties Nil. Weather Bad.	Nil
BOURGOGNE I.15.d.70.60.	9.11.18	9pm	At 7am orders received from Brigade to move. 8pm orders to move to I.13.d. Orders received at I.13.d. on arrival at I.13.d. Orders received to push on to BOURGOGNE. The Bridges over the river L'ESCAUT had been considerable time to negotiate but the battalion two transport got across by 3.30 p.m. and arrived at BOURGOGNE and were billeted there by 8.50 pm. The transport was held up owing to the pontoon bridge breaking down, but arrived at BOURGOGNE at midnight. Casualties Nil. Weather very cold.	Nil

November 1918

Army Form C. 2118.

WAR DIARY
36th Northumberland Fusiliers
INTELLIGENCE SUMMARY.

(Erase heading not required.)

Instructions regarding War Diaries and Intelligence Summaries are contained in F.S. Regs., Part II. and the Staff Manual respectively. Title pages will be prepared in manuscript.

Place	Date	Hour	Summary of Events and Information	Remarks and references to Appendices
ANVAING L.1.C. 10.40.	10.11.18	9 pm	At 2.30 a.m. orders received from Brigade to continue the advance. Instructions for Btn. to ANVAING, in L.1.C. as follows:- "Btn. will move as Bde. Reserve in following order. C. Coy. Adv. Guard, A. Coy. D. Coy. H.Q. Coy. Afternoon guard will then pass over road T. 16. a. at 0730 hours and move via FAUCHY - VALAINES - LA LAIE - CORDES - ANVAING. The Battn. arrived at ANVAING at 1400 hours and was billeted. Casualties Nil. Weather good.	Nil
do	11.11.18	9 pm	At 1300 hours wire from Bde. received. "Hostilities cease 1100 today. Brigade will not move today. No communication is to be held with the enemy." Casualties Nil. Weather good.	Nil
LEUZE.	12.11.18	9 pm	At 0430 hours following wire received from Bde. "you will move to LEUZE for work on Railway under A.D.G.T. Tomorrow Nov 12th. Billets from MAIRE or TOWN MAJOR LEUZE, Sheet 37. R.35.a. Commence work 13th." The Btn. moved off at 1100 hours and arrived in LEUZE at 1800 hours. The roads were very badly damaged by mines and this caused great delay. Btn. billeted. Casualties Nil. Weather good.	Nil
do.	13.11.18	"	Btn. resting.	

November 1918 3rd Bn Northumberland Fusiliers

Army Form C. 2118.

WAR DIARY
or
INTELLIGENCE SUMMARY.
(Erase heading not required.)

Instructions regarding War Diaries and Intelligence Summaries are contained in F. S. Regs. Part II. and the Staff Manual respectively. Title pages will be prepared in manuscript.

Place	Date	Hour	Summary of Events and Information	Remarks and references to Appendices
LEUZE	14.11.18	9 p.m.	Working parties were provided from Battalion for work on railway.	aww
"	15.11.18	9 p.m.	Inspection of Battalion by Brigade Commander at 10.45 a.m. held at R.34.b.5.2 (Sheet 37)	aww
"	16.11.18	9 p.m.	Continuation of working parties.	aww
"	17.11.18	9 p.m.	Divine Service (Voluntary) held in the CONVENT HALL at 11.00	aww
LEUZE — KAIN	18.11.18	9 p.m.	All instructions for working parties were cancelled and Battalion was instructed to hold themselves in readiness to move. Battalion proceeded by route march to KAIN at 09.30 hrs. Billets in KAIN were occupied during night 18th/19th	aww
KAIN — TEMPLEUVE	19.11.18	9 p.m.	Battalion proceeded by route march to TEMPLEUVE, resting in TEMPLEUVE during night 19th/20th	aww
TEMPLEUVE — PETIT RONCHIN	20.11.18	9 p.m.	Battalion proceeded by route march to PETIT RONCHIN (LILLE) at 08.30 hrs and were billeted in that area on arrival. Battalion rejoined 178 Inf Brigade Group.	aww

November 1918

WAR DIARY
or
INTELLIGENCE SUMMARY.

26th Northumberland Fusiliers

Army Form C. 2118.

Place	Date	Hour	Summary of Events and Information	Remarks and references to Appendices
PETIT RONCHIN	21/11/18	9 a.m.	Battalion today at PETIT RONCHIN. Inspection was held under Company arrangements. Notification of the following awards received:— The Military Cross 2/Lt A Woodward Northumberland Fusiliers. The Distinguished Conduct Medal 79024 Pte (L/Cpl) E FOULKES Northd Fusiliers 316318 Pte CLARK C.H. "	Asn
"	22/11/18	9 a.m.	Medical Inspection of A & B Coys. Preliminary arrangements were made in view of education scheme. Football continues.	Asn
"	23/11/18	9 a.m.	Tea afternoon reorganizing together for	Asn
"	24/11/18	9 a.m.	Brigade Thanksgiving Service held in field near Templemars at 11.00 hrs	Asn

November 1918

WAR DIARY
or
INTELLIGENCE SUMMARY.
(Erase heading not required.)

Army Form C. 2118.

26th Northumberland Fusiliers

Place	Date	Hour	Summary of Events and Information	Remarks and references to Appendices
PETIT RONCHIN	25/11/18	9 p.m.	Training carried out on parade ground during morning. Football match played in afternoon. Weather fair.	Appx.
	26/11/18	9 p.m.	Brigade road in parade ground. Inspection of men who have recently joined detachments and carried out by A.P.M.	Appx.
	27/11/18	2/00	G.O.C. Dinner. Weather fine. Training carried out on parade ground during morning. Football match played in afternoon. Weather fine.	Appx.
	28		General Holiday. There was a 3 mile cross country race in the morning. Sports which were arranged for the day weren't carried out owing to bad weather.	Appx.
	29		Bathing was carried out during the morning. In the afternoon, owing to inclement weather the sports were again unpossible.	
	30	0900	Two hours training in the afternoon & morning. In the afternoon football. Evening — Battalion Concert.	

J.P. Thompson
Lieut Col
Cmdg 26th Bn NORTHD FUSILIERS.

THE GAP BETWEEN NOVEMBER 1918 AND MAY 1919 HAS BEEN NOTED

36TH BATTN.
NORTHUMBERLAND
FUSILIERS.

WAR DIARY.

MAY. 1919.

36TH BATTALION NORTHUMBERLAND FUSILIERS

MAY 1919.

WAR DIARY
or
INTELLIGENCE SUMMARY
(Erase heading not required.)

Army Form C. 2118.

Place	Date	Hour	Summary of Events and Information	Remarks and references to Appendices
DUNKERQUE	MAY 1919		Location and Establishment — During the month of May, the Battalion continued to perform duties as "Marching in" Demobilisation" Staffing two Embarkation Camps and providing detachments for Concentration Camps R.O.D. Locks Etc. in Dunkerque and district.	
			Reinforcements — Officers —, Other Ranks 25	
			Demobilised from Battn. Officers 1, Other Ranks 18	

Army Form C. 2118.

MAY 1913

WAR DIARY
or
INTELLIGENCE SUMMARY.
(Erase heading not required.)

Place	Date	Hour	Summary of Events and Information	Remarks and references to Appendices
DUNKERQUE	MAY 1913		Strength of Bath. Officers 43 Other Ranks 1,060	
			Total number of Officers 361 troops passed through Other Ranks 13,058 during Month	
			Training. Towards the end of the month Donkirk demand to such an extent that No 2 Company asked for the purpose. Shown that the Bath to receive training of Grenade and Bomb the in addition to the N.C.O. class of Instructors which had been carried on all along.	

J. Nixon. Lieut. Colonel
Comdg. 36th Bn. Northumberland Fusiliers.

www.ingramcontent.com/pod-product-compliance
Lightning Source LLC
Chambersburg PA
CBHW081444160426
43193CB00013B/2378